whitney vs characters
are both
a political
influence

Whitney
vs Queen = emotional anchor

The Life and Death of Political

Jack Straw ✗ Influence

An anonymous play of the sixteenth century

Political reform
fairer laws for
the lower class

Edited for the Groundling Press,
and with an introduction by
Christopher Hapka

Table of Contents

About the Groundling Press

The Groundling Press publishes useful, readable, affordable e-book and on-demand editions of English-language plays from the sixteenth, seventeenth, and early eighteenth centuries for general readers and practical performers. Each play has been newly and carefully edited from one or more early printed texts or manuscripts. These editions are not based on any existing public-domain text.

The plays have been newly modernized from the original old-spelling texts, with the intention of creating a text that is readable and accessible to a modern reader. Spelling has been updated to conform to modern usage; however, archaic forms have been retained where they affect pronunciation or meter. Punctuation has likewise been silently modernized. Notes are provided for words and references that may be unfamiliar to the modern reader, and appendices provide interesting materials related to the text, where available.

To keep the plays affordable, they are currently available only in e-book and print-on-demand editions. Performance rights to this modernized edition are available at no charge or at a nominal fee, but permission must be sought in advance. Please visit our web site, www.groundlingpress.com, for more information.

Jack Straw and the Peasants' Revolt

The Peasants' Revolt of 1381

The turbulent year of 1381 changed English history, and the history of Europe. In what we now call the "Peasants' Revolt," tens of thousands of poor men and women from Essex and Kent, led by peasants known as Wat Tyler and Jack Straw, marched on London in protest of the conditions they endured as feudal serfs.

The Peasants' Revolt followed close on the heels of the Black Death, which killed between a quarter and a half of the English population in 1348 and 1349, then struck again in 1360. A feudal system dependent on cheap, plentiful labor began to show signs of strain as land went unworked. The government passed harsh laws setting maximum payment for labor at its pre-plague value.

The plague also affected tax revenues. With less revenue coming in from ordinary taxes and tariffs, the government began to levy a series of poll taxes, individual taxes paid per head, in order to pay for the ongoing campaigns of the Hundred Years' War. In 1377 and 1379, each English man and woman had to pay a flat tax of at least fourpence, in a time when a family might earn less than a penny a day.

Then, in late 1380, a third poll tax was introduced, to be collected in 1381. This time, the tax was increased from four pence to twelve pence in pre-decimal money, per head, for everyone, rich or poor. A family of three, who might earn fifteen or twenty pence in a month, would owe thirty-six pence in taxes, on top of the normal tithes and duties owed to their feudal lords. Adding to the insult, unlike the 1379 tax, the 1381 tax was not graduated by income, so rich lords and ladies had to pay the same pennies as the poorest ploughman.

The Peasants' Revolt escalated from protests against this tax, where townspeople banded together to expel or attack tax collectors. By the end, tens of thousands of serfs and townspeople had captured the Tower of London and killed many of the politicians responsible for the tax. John of Gaunt, the richest man in England and a public figure closely associated with the tax, escaped only by fleeing to Scotland. His palace at the Savoy, the most visible symbol of the wealth and power of the nobility, was burnt to the ground.

The revolt was put down, and the leaders killed, but it had served its purpose. No new poll tax was levied in England for more than 250 years, and serfdom quickly declined and was replaced by less oppressive feudal forms.

Shakespeare never wrote a play about the Peasants' Revolt, but its influence is felt in his histories. King Richard II was personally associated with the suppression of the revolt and the death of Wat Tyler and Jack Straw. Twenty years later, he was deposed in another revolt, this one led by the son of John of Gaunt. When Gaunt's grandson, Henry V, needed funds, Parliament turned to wealthy church institutions instead of to the peasantry; it is this threat that the priests discuss in the opening scene of Shakespeare's play.

The Peasants' Revolt has resonance even today. In 1990, when Margaret Thatcher tried to bring the poll tax back to modern Britain to replace the more progressive property tax system, protesters marched in opposition, intentionally following the route of Wat Tyler's armies.

Wat Tyler and Jack Straw

By the turn of the 17th century, Wat Tyler, John Ball, and Jack Straw would have been familiar from stories and ballads. The historical evidence for their lives, and in some cases their existence, is as scarce as would be expected of a medieval peasant. What we know of them comes from unreliable oral tradition and a handful of almost as unreliable, and much more one-sided, chroniclers. The play only adds to the confusion, as in the later acts, the part played by Jack Straw is universally assigned by the chroniclers to Wat Tyler, a fact that would have been well known to the audience.

The Life and Death of Jack Straw, at least on the surface, takes a straightforwardly royalist view of the Peasant's Revolt—as any play would have to do that wanted to be heard and seen in sixteenth-century London. But the playwright relies on the audience's knowledge of events to fill in some of the rebels' motivation.

This starts in the very first scene, where Straw becomes enraged at the royal tax collector for attempting

> To play so unmanly and beastly a part,
> As to search my daughter thus in my presence.

This refers to one story, from Holinshed's chronicle, of what triggered the uprising: that the tax collector responded to Straw's claim that his daughter was fourteen and thus exempt from the poll tax by molesting her, under the pretense of seeing if she had reached puberty. In this play, the actual assault apparently takes place offstage and before the action; Straw's daughter herself never appears. The scene makes sense, however, only if the audience already knows the story and can provide Straw's motivation for killing the tax collector.

There may be some subtle jokes at royal expense in the later acts as well. When the young Richard II swears "by all the honour of my Crown" that the rebels will be pardoned, the audience would likely have known that in fact these pardons were ignored or repealed, and leaders of the revolt executed throughout England.

About the Text

"Jack Straw" is an anonymous play, first printed in London in 1593 and reprinted in 1604. The current text is based on the 1604 edition, with reference to the 1593 first edition for certain passages. Both of these editions are divided into acts, but not scenes. To aid modern readers and performers, this editor has added scene divisions at natural breaks in the action.

The word "taske" is used throughout the play to mean "tax." For instance, Straw's first line, in the 1604 edition, reads:

art thou Collecter of the Kings Taske,

In the interest of readability, the word "tax" has been substituted throughout, although the rhyme-scheme of Act 1 Scene 1 indicates that it would have been pronounced to rhyme with "ask."

Dramatis Personae

A Tax Collector

Jack Straw

Wat Tyler

Tom Miller
a clown

Parson Ball

Nobs

The Lord Treasurer

The Archbishop of Canterbury

A Secretary

A Messenger

Hob Carter

The Queen Mother

The County of Salisbury

A Gentleman Usher

King Richard II

Sir John Morton

Sir John Newton

Spencer
a bargeman

A Fleming

The Lord Mayor of London

Rebels, Southwarkmen, Two Sergeants, Guards, Gentlemen, Noblemen

ACT ONE

Scene 1

Enter TAX COLLECTOR, JACK STRAW.

Collector. Now such a murmuring to rise upon so trifling a thing*
In all my life never saw I before,
And yet I have been officer this seven year and more.
The tiler* and his wife are in a great rage,
Affirming their daughter to be underage.*

Straw. Art thou collector of the king's tax?

Collector. I am, tiler, why dost thou ask?

Straw. Because thou goest beyond the commission of the king.
We grant his Highness' pleasure in everything:
Thou hast my tax money for all that be here,
My daughter is not fourteen years old, therefore she goes clear.

Collector. And because thou sayest so, I should believe thee?

---

so trifling a thing: The poll tax of 1381 was seen by the population as
oppressive and draconian. See the introduction for a discussion of the
impact of the tax and the play's positioning of the rebels and the royal
faction.

tiler: A laborer who made or repaired tiles, either for floors or roofs. In the
original, the collector says "Tyler" here and in his next line. In
Holinshed's *Chronicles*, the primary source for this episode, Holinshead
writes that Jack Straw's actual name was John Tyler, but that he called
himself "Jack Straw" when he became captain of the rebels.

underage: As Straw goes on to explain, children under a certain age were
exempt from the tax. As the tax per head may have been as high as two
weeks' wages for some serfs, the difference between paying two or three
heads of tax would be significant.

1

Straw.   Choose whether thou wilt or no, thou get'st no more of me,
              For I am sure thy office doth not arm thee with such authority
              Thus to abuse the poor people of the country.
              But chiefest of all, vile villains* as thou art,
              To play so unmanly and beastly a part,
              As to search my daughter thus in my presence.*

Collector. Why, base villain, wilt thou teach me what to do;
              Wilt thou prescribe me mine office, and what belongs thereto?

Straw.   What, villain, doth strike me? I swear by the rood,*
              As I am Jack Straw, thou shalt buy it with thy blood.

                    STRAW *kills the* COLLECTOR.

              There lie and be well paid for thy pain.

Collector. O, help, help, the king's officer is slain!

                    Enter PARSON BALL, WAT TYLER, NOBS,
                    and TOM MILLER *the clown.*

Tyler.   How now, Jack Straw, doth anybody abuse thee?

Straw.   Alas, Wat, I have killed the king's officer in striking rashly.

---

vile villains: The original text has "vilde villains." Throughout, "vilde" is
    rendered as "vile," though there are some places where "wild" would be
    just as appropriate.

to search my daughter thus: The outrage is apparently meant to have
    happened offstage, before the play began. The playwright may have
    depended on the audience being familiar with Holinshed's account, in
    which, on hearing that the girl was underage, the collector replies that, as
    girls of fourteen or fifteen "have commonly hair growing forth about
    [their] private parts," he would "feel whether her daughter were of lawful
    age or not, and therewith began to misuse the maid, and search further
    than honesty would have permitted."

rood: The cross.

2

Miller.   A small matter to recover a man that is slain,
            Blow wind in his tail and fetch him again.

Ball.   Content thee, 'tis no matter, and Jack Straw, god-a-mercy,
            Herein thou hast done good service to thy country.
            Were all inhuman slaves so served as he,
            England would be civil, and from all such dealings free.

Tyler.* By Gog's blood,* my masters, we will not put up this* so
                quietly,
            We owe God a death and we can but die:
            And though the fairest end of a rebel is the gallows,
            Yet if you will be ruled by me,
            We'll so deal of ourselves as we'll revenge this villainy.

Straw.   The king, God wot,* knows not what's done by such poor men
                as we,
            But we'll make him know it, if you will be ruled* by me:

Tyler: The printer gives this line to Nobs, but this appears to be a mistake. It is inconsistent with Nobs' line at the end of the scene, where he introduces himself as the captains' boy and expresses doubt as to the revolution's success. In that line, he even quotes and mocks a line from this one ("ye hear them say they owe God a death, and they can but die"). Assigning this line to Tyler makes more sense; otherwise, Tyler, the most famous of the rebels, would have almost no role in the initial conspiracy or in the opening scene of the play. In addition, the oath "Gog's blood" appears three more times in the play, each time spoken by Tyler.

By Gog's blood: A "minced oath" version of "By God's blood," with Gog, a name used in several parts of the Bible, replacing God to make the saying sound less offensive or sacreligious. This may have been done by the printer, by the censor, or by the playwright. The reference to Gog probably has no particular meaning, but does carry some apocalypic overtones from its use in the Book of Revelation.

put up this: Put up with this; alternatively, put this away.

wot: Knows.

ruled: Guided.

Here's Parson Ball, honest priest, and tells us that in charity,[*]
We may stick together in such quarrels honestly.

Miller What, is he an honest man? The devil he is, he is the parson of
          the town.
You think there's no knavery hid under a black gown?[*]
Find him in a pulpit but twice in the year,
And I'll find him forty times in the alehouse, tasting strong
          beer.

[handwritten: Negative Introduction — Setting Patriotic terms]

Ball. Neighbors, neighbors, the weakest nowadays goes to the wall.[*]
But mark my words and follow the counsel of John Ball:
England is grown to such a pass of late,
That rich men triumph[*] to see the poor beg at their gate.
But[*] I am able by good scripture before you to prove
That God doth not this dealing allow nor love.
But when Adam delved, and Eve span,
Who was then a gentleman?[*]
Brethren, brethren, it were better to have this community
Than to have this difference in degrees,
The landlord his rent, the lawyer his fees,
So quickly the poor man's substance is spent;
But merrily with the world it went

[handwritten: reassurance that the oppressed should be dealt with]

[handwritten: Slogan of rebellion]

---

in charity: Consistently with Christian love or Christian doctrine.

black gown: Priestly vestments.

goes to the wall: Dies or fails; cf. Romeo and Juliet, I.i. ("That shows thee a
weak slave; for the weakest goes to the wall.")

triumph: Gloat.

But: On the contrary.

when Adam delved and Eve span / Who was then a gentleman?: This
line was reported by chroniclers as a rallying cry for the rebels, and the
subject of the historical John Ball's most famous sermon, one account of
which is included as an appendix to this edition. To delve is to dig, and
"span" refers to spinning thread, both menial tasks. Ball is asking, if God
did not create lords and serfs in the Garden of Eden, but had Adam and
Eve do their own labor, why there is such a division in the modern
world.

[handwritten: There is no difference in decree no gentlemen]

4

When men ate berries of the hawthorne tree,
And "if thou help me, I'll help thee."
There was no place for surgery
And old men knew not usury.
The widow that hath but a pan of brass,
And scarce a house to hide her head,
Sometimes no penny to buy her bread,
Must pay her landlord many a groat,*
Or 'twill be pull'd out of her throat.
Brethren, mind, so might I thrive,
As I wish not to be alive
To see such dealings with extremity*—
The rich have all, the poor live in misery.
But follow the counsel of John Ball,
I promise you, I love ye all,
And make division equally
Of each man's goods indifferently,
And rightly may you follow arms
To rid you from these civil harms.

Straw.   Well said, parson. May it be.
As we purpose to prefer,
We will have all the rich men displaced,
And all the bravery of them defaced.
And as rightly as I am Jack Straw,
In spite of all the men of law,
Make thee Archbishop of Canterbury,
And Chancellor of England,* or I'll die.
How saith thou, Wat, shall it be so?

---

groat: A fourpenny coin. The tax Straw is protesting was three groats a person.

extremity: Poverty.

Chancellor of England: At the time, the titles of Archbishop of Canterbury and Lord Chancellor were held by the same man, the much-hated Simon Sutcliffe.

Tyler.	Aye, Jack Straw, or else I'll bide* many a foul blow.
	It shall be no other but he,
	That thus favours the commonalty.*
	Stay we no longer prating here,
	But let us roundly to this gear.*
	'Tis more than time that we were gone,
	We'll be lords, my masters, every one.
Miller.	And I, my masters, will make one
	To fight when all our foes be done.
	Well shall they see, before we'll lack,
	We'll stuff the gallows 'till it crack.
Straw.	I hope we shall have men enow,
	To aid us herein. Wat, how thinkest thou?
Ball.	Tag and rag* thou need'st not doubt.
Tyler.	But who shall be captain of the rout?
Ball.	That shall you two for all our Kentish men.
Straw.	Fellow captain, welcome; let's about it.
Tyler.	Agreed, fellow captains: to London!

Exit all but NOBS.

Nobs.	Here's even work towards for the hangman. Did you ever see such a crew?
	After so bad a beginning, what's like to ensue?

---

bide: Endure.

commonalty: Common people; what elsewhere in the play is called the "commons."

gear: Stuff; things.

Tag and rag: The rabble.

6

Faith, even the common reward for rebels, swingledom
    swangledom,* you know as well as I.
But what care they? Ye hear them say they owe God a death,
    and they can but die;
'Tis dishonour for such as they to die in their bed,
And credit to caper* under the gallows, all save the head.*
And yet, by my fay,* the beginning of this riot
May chance cost many a man's life before all be quiet;
And i'faith, I'll be amongst them as forward as the best,
And if ought fall out but well,* I shall shift* amongst the rest,
And being but a boy, may hide me in the throng.
Tyburn,* stand fast, I fear you will be laden ere it be long.

Exit NOBS.

---

swingledom swangledom: Hanging.

caper: Dance.

save the head: Except for their heads. Nobs is saying that when the rebels are hanged, all of their bodies except their heads will be "dancing" on the gallows.

by my fay: In faith; *cf.* Chaucer, The Reeve's Tale.

if ought fall out but well: As long as things go well.

shift: Make do; get by. The implication is that Nobs intends to survive by taking advantage of the chaos of the revolt.

Tyburn: The "Tyburn tree" in Marylebone was a large gallows, built in 1571, where mass executions of up to 20 people at a time were carried out.

7

Scene 2

Enter the LORD TREASURER,* *the* ARCHBISHOP OF CANTERBURY,* *and* SECRETARY,* *with others.*

Treasurer. And yet, Lord Archbishop, your Grace doth know
That since the latest time of Parliament,*
Wherein this tax was granted to the king
By general consent of either house,
To help his wars which he intends to France,
For wreak* and just revovery of his right,
How slow their payment is in every place;
That better a king not to command at all,
Than be beholding to ungrateful minds.

Archbishop. Lord Treasurer, it seemeth strange to me
That being won with reason and regard
Of true succeeding* Prince, the common sort

[handwritten: Kings cannot tax without their consent]

Lord Treasurer: In 1381, the Lord Treasurer of England was Robert Hales. As the official directly responsible for collecting the poll tax, he was hated by the rebels.

Archbishop of Canterbury: In 1381, Simon Sutcliffe was Archbishop of Canterbury and Lord Chancellor of England. As Lord Chancellor, the rebels blamed him as well as the Lord Treasurer for the poll tax, making him one of the most hated men in England.

Secretary: The 1593 and 1604 printings simply call this character "Secretary." The reference may be to the King's Secretary, a high official. Around the time of the Peasants' Revolt, this office was held by Robert Braybrook and John Bacon.

time of Parliament: In the fourteenth century, the parliament met only once or twice a year, when summoned, during which any legislative business would have had to take place. The parliament that authorized the 1381 poll tax met from November 5 to December 6, 1380.

wreak: Revenge, punishment.

true succeeding: Legitimate; not a usurper.

Should be so slack* to give, or grudge* the gift,
That is to be employed for their behoofe.*
Hard and unnatural be the thoughts of theirs
[That suck the milk, and will not help the weal.*]
The king himself being now but young of age,*
If things should fall out otherwise than well,
The blame doth fall upon the counselor,
And if I take my aim not all awry,
[The multitude, a beast of many heads,] —common troupe
Of misconceiving and misconstruing minds,*
Reputes* this last benevolence* to the king,
Given at the high court of Parliament,
A matter more required for private good,
Than help or benefit of common weal.*
Wherein how much they wrong the better sort,
My conscience beareth witness, in the cause.

Secretary.   My Lords, because your words not worthless are;
Because they stand on reason's surest ground,
And tend unto the profit of the king
Whose profit is the profit of the land,
Yet give me leave, in reverence of the cause,

---

slack: Slow.

grudge: Begrudge.

behoof: Advantage.

weal: The welfare of the community. The 1593 edition has "VVell," and the 1604 text has "wel," which W.C. Hazlitt in his edition interpreted as "well." "Weal" or some similar sense seems a more likely reading.

young of age: At the time of the Peasants' Revolt in 1381, Richard II was fourteen years old.

Of misconceiving and misconstruing minds: This line is omitted from the 1604 edition, apparently because of a printer's error.

reputes: Considers.

benevolence: Generosity.

weal: Welfare.

To speak my mind touching this question.
When such as we do see the people's hearts,
Expres'd as far as time will give them leave,
With heartiness of their benevolence,
Methinks it were for others' happiness
That hearts and purses should together go:
Misdeem* not, good my Lords, of this my speech;
Sith* well I wot* the noble and the slave,
And all doth have but for a common weal,*
Which common weal, in other terms, is the king's.

Enter a MESSENGER.

Messenger.   The justices and sheriffs of Kent send greetings to your
                    Honours here by me.

Archbishop (reading). My Lords, this brief* doth openly unfold,
                    A dangerous tax* to us and all our trains.
                    With speed let us impart the news unto my lord the king,
                    The fearful news, that* while the flame doth but begin,
                    Sad policy* may serve to quench the fire:
                    The commons now are up in Kent, let us not suffer this first
                          attempt too far.

---

misdeem: Misunderstand.

Sith: Since.

wot: Know, understand.

doth have but for a common weal: Are (or should be) working for a
    common good.

brief: Writing; written summary. Here it refers to the paper brought by the
    Messenger.

tax: Demand. In the original this is "taske," the same term used for the poll
    tax; it might just as well in this context be modernized to "task."

that: So that.

Sad policy: Serious and steadfast political efforts.

10

Treasurer   My friend, what power* have they assembled in the field?

Messenger.   My lord, a twenty thousand men or there about.

Secretary.   See here the peril that was late* foreseen, *This rebellion was predicted*
Ready to fall on this unhappy land. *Turmoil / suffering*
What barbarous minds, for grievance more than needs,*
Unnaturally seek wreak* upon their lord, *The common are viewed*
Their true anounted prince, their lawful king; *as barbaric*
So dare this blind unshamefac'd multitude *Seeking revenge*
Lay violent* hands they wot* not why nor where. *against king*
But be thou still as best becometh thee,
To stand in quarrel with thy natural liege—
The sun may sometimes be eclips'd with clouds,
But hardly may the twinkling stars obscure,
Or put him out, of whom they borrow light.*   *His authority is like the Sun. Always Prevail*

All exit.

Rebels

---

what power: How many (armed) men?

late: Recently; just.

for grievance more than needs: Because of annoyances rather than necessities.

wreak: Revenge, punishment.

violent: Involving physical force.

wot: Know, understand.

him...of whom they borrow light: Some prominent natural philosophers of the middle ages, including Albertus Magnus, believed that the stars only reflected or redirected the light of the sun.

Scene 3

Enter JACK STRAW, WAT TYLER, HOB CARTER, TOM
MILLER, *and* NOBS.

Straw.	Aye, marry, Wat, this is another matter; methinks the world is changed of late.
	Who would live like a beggar, and* may be in this estate?*
Tyler.	We are here four captains just, Jack Straw, Wat Tyler, Hob Carter, and Tom Miller.
	Search me all England and find four such Captains, and, by Gog's blood,* I'll be hang'd.
Nobs (aside).	So you will be nevertheless, I stand in great doubt.*
Carter.	Captain Straw, and Captain Tyler, I think I have brought a company of Essex men for my train,
	That will never yield,* but kill or else be slain.
Miller.	And for a little captain I have the 'vantage* of you all,
	For while you are a-fighting, I can creep into a quart-pot, I am so small.
Nobs.	But, masters, what answer made Sir John Morton* at Rochester?

---

and: If he; even if he.

estate: Condition.

by Gog's blood: See note to Act 1 Scene 1.

I stand in great doubt: Nobs is expressing doubt of the enterprise; he is confident that Tyler will be hanged.

yield: Surrender.

'vantage: Advantage.

Sir John Morton: The story of John Morton's capture by the rebels is from Grafton's *Chronicle*. Grafton reports that when the rebels took Rochester, they told Morton, who was the local lord, that he, on pain of death,

	I heard say he would keep the castle still, for the king's use.
Straw.	So he did till I fetch'd him out by force, and I have his wife and children pledges* for his speedy return from the king, to whom he is gone with our message.
Miller.	Let him take heed he bring a wise answer to our worships, or else his pledges goes to the pot.*
Carter.	Captain Straw, how many men have we in the field?
Straw.	Marry, captain Carter, about fifty thousand men.
Carter.	Where shall we pitch our tents to lie in safety?
Straw.	Marry, Hob, upon Blackheath beside Greenwich, there we'll lie. And if the king will come thither to know our pleasures so it is, if no, I know what we'll do.
Tyler.	Gog's blood, Jack, have we the cards in our hands? Let's take it upon us* while we have it.

Exit all but NOBS.

Nobs.	Aye, marry, for you know not how long you shall hold it.

"must go with us, and be our sovereign captain, and do that we will have you do." Froissart's Chronicle gives this same role to Sir John Newton, who appears later in the play.

pledges: Hostages.

goes to the pot: An earlier form of the modern expression "go to pot." The origin of the phrase is obscure; it may refer to the pit, or pot, of Hell; or to the practice of chopping up old scraps of meat for stew. Miller is likely punning on another possible origin of the phrase: the idea that a metal item "pledged" at the pawnbroker's shop would be put into the pawnbroker's melting pot if the pledge was not redeemed.

take it upon us: Take the initiative.

Fifty thousand men they have already in arms that will draw
    together.
If we hang together as fast, some of us shall repent it.

Exit NOBS.

Scene 4

Enter the QUEEN MOTHER, *the* COUNTY OF SALISBURY,* *and*
a GENTLEMAN USHER.

Queen Mother. This strange welcome and unhappy news
        Of these unnatural rebels and unjust,
        That threaten wrack unto this wretched land,
        Aye me! affrights my woman's mazed* mind,
        Burdens my heart, and interrupts my sleep,
        That* now unless some better tidings come,
        Unto my son their true anointed king,
        My heavy heart I fear will break in twain,
        Surcharged* with a heavy load of thoughts.

Salisbury.   Madam, your grace's care in this I much commend,
        For though your son, my lord the king, be young,
        Yet he will see so well unto himself*
        That he will make the proudest* rebel know
        What 'tis to move* or to displease a king.
        And though his looks bewray* such lenity,*

County of Salisbury: "Count" or "County" was a title of nobility in medieval
    England. It has since been replaced with "Earl," although an earl's wife
    still retains the title "Countess."

mazed: Confused, bewildered.

That: So that.

Surcharged: Burdened, weighted down.

see so well unto himself: Look after himself so well.

proudest: Bravest.

move: Excite the passions of.

bewray: Disclose; display.

lenity: Mercy.

15

Yet at advantage* he can use extremity.*
Your Grace may call to mind that, being a king,
He will not put up* any injury;
Especially of* base and common men,
Which are not worthy but* with reverence
To look into the princely state of kings.
A king sometimes will make a show of courtesy
Only to fit a following policy;*
And it may be the king determines so
That he will try before he trust a foe.

Usher.   True, Madam, for your grace's son, the king,
Is so well ruled* by divers* of his peers
As that I think the proudest foe he hath
Shall find more work than he will take in hand,
That seeks the downfall of his Majesty.
I hope the council are too wise for that*
To suffer rebels in aspiring pride
That purpose treason to the prince and state.
In good time,* see where my lord the king
Doth come, accompanied with the bishop* and Lord
    Treasurer.

---

at advantage: When it is to his advantage.

extremity: Extreme measures.

put up: Put up with.

of: At the hands of.

but: Except.

policy: Stratagem.

ruled: Guided; influenced.

divers: Of various kinds.

too wise for that: Too wise to.

In good time: At a suitable or appropriate time.

bishop / Archbishop of Canterbury: In the 1593 and 1604 texts, this character, who has several lines in the enuing scene, is designated as simply "Bishop," whereas the Archbishop of Canterbury is designated

Enter the KING, *the* ARCHBISHOP OF CANTERBURY, *and the*
LORD TREASURER.

King.　　　I marvel much, my Lords, what rage it is
　　　　　That moves my people, whom I love so dear,
　　　　　Under a show* of quarrel good and just
　　　　　To rise against us thus in mutinies,
　　　　　With threat'ning force against our state and us.
　　　　　But if it be as we are given to know,
　　　　　By letters and by credible report,
　　　　　A little spark hath kindled all this fire,
　　　　　Which must be quench'd with circumspect regard,
　　　　　Before we feel the violence* of the flame.
　　　　　Meanwhile, sweet lady mother, be content,
　　　　　And think* their malice shall not injure you.
　　　　　For we have tools to crop and cut them off
　　　　　Ere they presume to touch our royal self;
　　　　　And thus resolve, that you secure shall be,
　　　　　What hard* mishap soever fall to me.

Enter SIR JOHN MORTON*

"Archbishop" earlier in the act. However, given that Hales, the Lord
Treasurer, and Sutcliffe, the Archbishop, appear together elsewhere in
the play, and that they were associated together in the public mind, it
seems likely that he is intended here, as well. The difference may be due
to a different hand setting the type for this section of the play, or because
this section was copied from a different source. In either case, this
edition assumes that this scene's bishop, who appears nowhere else in the
play, is also meant to represent Archbishop Sutcliffe. The accompanying
stage direction has been added by this editor; no clarifying stage direction
appears in either the 1593 or 1604 editions.

show: Pretense or pretext.

violence: Power; force.

think: Believe; hold the opinion that.

hard: Severe; painful; violent.

Morton.	Health and good hap* befall your Majesty.
Usher.	My lord, here is a messenger from Kent,
	That craves* access unto your Majesty.
King.	Admit him near, for we will hear him speak.
	'Tis hard when, 'twixt the people and the king,
	Such terms of threats and parleys* must be had.
	Would any gentleman or man of worth
	Be seen in such a cause without offence,
	Both to his God, his country, and his prince,
	Except they were enforced* thereunto?
Queen Mother.	I cannot think so good a gentleman
	As is that knight, Sir John Morton, I mean,
	Would entertain so base and vile* a thought;
	Nor can it sink into my woman's head
	That, were it not for fear or policy,*
	So true a bird would foul so fair a nest.
	But here he comes; O, so my longing mind
	Desires to know the tidings he doth bring.

Enter Sir John Morton: In both the 1593 and 1604 printings, the direction here reads "Enter Messenger," and no attribution is given for the following line, here assigned to Morton. Given that the king describes Morton in his next line, and the queen mother refers to him by name, the playwright may have intended that Morton enter as the messenger and be visible on the stage during both speeches. As an alternative, in performance, Morton's first line may be delivered by another messenger, and the Usher may give the king and queen mother a note identifying Morton, who would then enter at the Queen's line, "here he comes."

good hap: Good fortune.

craves: Earnestly seeks.

parleys: Conferences, usually between enemies.

enforced: Compelled by force; forced.

vile: See note to Act 1 Scene 1.

policy: Stratagem.

Morton. The Commons of Kent salute your majesty,
And I am made their unhappy messenger:
My Lord, a crew* of rebels are in field,
And they have made commotions late in Kent,
And drawn your people to a mutiny:
And if your Grace see not to it in time,
Your land will come to ruin by their means.
Yet may your Grace find remedy in time,
To qualify* their pride that thus presume.

Archbishop. Who are the captains of this rebel rout
That thus do rise 'gainst their anointed king?
What, be they men of any worth or no?
If men of worth, I cannot choose but pity them.

Morton. No, my good lord, they be men of no great account.
For they be none but tilers, thatchers, millers, and such like,
That in their lines did never come in field*
Before this mutiny did call them forth:
And for security of my back return,*
Upon this message which I show'd the king,
They keep my wife and children for a pledge,*
And hal'd me out from forth my castle at Rochester,
And swore me* there to come unto your Majesty;
And having told you their minds,
I hope your Grace will pardon me for all,
In that I am enforced* thereunto.

[handwritten: Regular men]
[handwritten: Rebel]

---

crew: A company of armed men.

qualify: Mitigate; lessen.

That in their lines did never come in field: They have never been part of a
  regular army.

for security of my back return: To ensure that I will go back to them.

pledge: A security deposit, as at a pawnbroker's.

swore me: Made me swear an oath.

enforced: Compelled by force; forced.

King.	How many men have they assembled in the field?
Morton.	I think, my lord, about twenty thousand men.
	But if your Grace would follow my advice,
	Thus would I deal with these rebellious men:
	I would find time to parley* with some of them,
	And know what in their minds they do intend.
	For being armed with such treacherous thoughts,
	They may perform more than your Grace expects.

King.

↓
Response

With speed return to these unnatural men,
And see, Sir John, you greet them thus from me:
Tell them that we ourself will come to them
To understand their meaning and their minds,*
And tell them, if they have any evil sustain'd,*
Ourself will see sufficient recompense.
Go, good Sir John, and tell them upon the Thames
Our self will meet with them,
There to confer concerning their avail.*
Do so, Sir John, and kindly recommend* us to them all.

Morton.	We shall fulfill your Grace's mind in this.
	And thus I take my conge* of your Majesty,
	Wishing your Grace thrice Nestor's years* to reign,
	To keep* your land, and guard your royal train.*

---

parley: Talk; negotiate.

their meaning and their minds: Their intentions.

sustain'd: Suffered.

avail: Benefit; advantage; may also carry the sense of effort or struggle.

recommend: Send greetings; literally, entrust us to them.

conge: To politely take leave; to bow upon departure.

Nestor's years: In Greek mythology, and especially in the Iliad and Odyssey, Nestor was the famously wise and long-lived king of Pylos who sailed in the Argo with Jason and fought on the Greek side in the Trojan war.

keep: Safeguard; protect.

train: Followers; retainers; dependents.

Queen Mother. Farewell good knight, and as thou dare'st, remember them,*
though they forget themselves.

E   ON.

Archbishop. [Your Grace herein is   ed
With resolution fitting y
Your Grace must show yo   a king,
And rule like God's viceregent   earth;
The looks of kings do lend both life a   death,
And when a king doth set down his decre
His sentence should be irrecovable.]
Your Grace herein hath shown your princely mind,
In that you hate to prey on carrion flesh:*
Such prey befits not kings to prey upon
That may command and countermand their own.
I hope, my Lord, this message so will prove*
That public hate will turn to private love.
And therefore I say, my Lord, you have answered well:
The tax was given your Grace by act of Parliament
And you have reason to demand your due.

King. My Lords, I hope we shall not need to fear
To meet those men that thus do threaten us.
We will, my lords, tomorrow meet with them
And hear, my lords, what 'tis that they demand.
Mother, your Grace shall need to take no care,
For you shall in our Tower of London stay*
Till we return from Kent to you again.
My Lord, see every thing prepar'd for us,

[handwritten annotation: encouraging King to compare life and death w the rest of the realm]

---

remember them: Remind them (of their duties).

viceregent: Viceroy; a monarch's representative in the monarch's absence.

carrion flesh: Dead animals, eaten only by scavengers.

prove: Turn out (in the end).

you shall in our Tower of London stay: The audience would understand this to be an ironic reference to the sacking of the Tower of London, which is not otherwise mentioned in the play.

And, mother, thus I leave your Majesty:
You to the tower and I must hence to Kent.

Treasurer. My Lord, if so you please take my advice herein,
That speaks in love and duty to your Grace,
I shall in every matter privilege* your Majesty and all your
      lordly train.
I mean against* your manor of Greenwich town
And so* amidst the stream may hover safe;
Meanwhile they send some few and chosen men
To give your Grace to understand their minds:
And thus, my Lord, I have adventured
To show your Majesty my mind herein.

---

privilege: Give a benefit or advantage to.

against: Close by.

And so: There may be one or more lines missing between the previous line
and this one, in which, presumably, the Lord Treasurer suggests that the
king take a barge to meet the rebels at Greenwich, as seen in Act 2.

ACT TWO

Scene 1

Enter TOM MILLER *with a goose.*

Miller It is good to make precaution, for peradventure* we shall lack victuals an* we lie in camps on Blackheath long. And in faith, as long as this goose lasts we'll not starve, and as many good fellows as will come to the eating of her, come and welcome. For in faith I came lightly by her, and lightly come lightly gone. We captains are lords within ourselves,*
And if the world hold out* we shall be kings shortly.

Enter NOBS, *who cuts away the goose* while he talketh, and exits, leaving the head behind him.*

Miller. The rest of my fellow Captains are gone before to Greenwich to meet the king, that comes to know our minds, and while they be about it:
I'll make good cheer, with my goose here—
What! is the goose flown away without her head?

Exit MILLER.

---

peradventure: It may happen that.

an: If. "And" in the original.

within ourselves: In our own minds.

if the world hold out: If all goes well.

cuts away the goose: Miller is presumably holding the goose by the neck, when Nobs enters, cuts the body away from the head, and takes the body; Miller only notices this before his last line. The original stage direction is somewhat confusing; it states "leue the head behinde him with them & Morton," although during this scene Miller is apparently alone on the stage.

23

Scene 2

Enter with the crew TOM MILLER,* JACK STRAW, WAT TYLER, *and* HOB CARTER.

Straw.   Here's a stir* more than needs!
             What means the king thus to abuse* us,
             And make us run about his pleasure, and to no end.*
             He promised us to meet us on the water,
             And, by Lady, as soon as we came at the waterside
             He fair and flat* turns his barge, and away he goes to London.
             I tell thee, Wat, we will not put up this abuse.

Tyler.   By Gog's blood,* Captain Straw, we will remove* our camp,
                and away to London roundly,*
             And there we'll speak with him, or we'll know why we shall
                not.

Straw.   God-a-mercy,* Wat, and ere we have done,
             We will be lords every one.

Tom Miller: Miller has just exited, after saying that all of his fellow captains were "gone before to Greenwich." He has no lines in this scene, and it is not clear whether he is really meant to be on stage or if this is a printer's error.

stir: Incitement to movement or action.

abuse: In addition to the modern meaning of "wrong" or "insult," may imply "deceive" or "trick".

to no end: With no purpose; unproductively.

fair and flat: This phrase emphasizes the intentional nature of the king's action.

by Gog's blood: See note to Act 1 Scene 1.

remove: Break camp and leave.

roundly: Quickly; directly.

God-a-mercy: An oath indicating approval or gratitude.

Carter.	Gentle Jack Straw, in one line let us draw,*
	And we'll not leave a man of law
	Nor a paper worth a haw,*
	And make him worser than a daw*
	That shall stand against Jack Straw.
Morton.	Methinks you might as well to answer the king,
	In the name of the whole company,
	Some dozen or twenty men for the nonce, that may deliver the
	minds of you all in few words.
Straw.	Sir John Morton, you are an ass, to tell us what we have to do;
	Hold your prating* you were best.
Tyler.	I tell thee, Sir John, thou abuse us.
	But let's to London, as fast as we can.

----

in one line let us draw: I.e., let us form a line of battle; let us fight together.

haw: A hawthorne berry; used as a type of something worthless.

daw: Literally, a jackdaw; figuratively, a simpleton or fool.

prating: Empty chatter.

Scene 3

Enter KING, ARCHBISHOP, LORD TREASURER,
SECRETARY, SIR JOHN NEWTON,* *and* SPENCER, *a bargeman*

King.*   My lords, if all our men are come unto the shore
       Let us return again into the town.
       These people are not to be talk'd withal,*
       Much less with reason to be ordered,*
       That so unorderly with shrikes* and cries
       Make show* as though they would invade* us all.
       I have not heard nor read of any king
       So ungently* of his people entertain'd.*

Exit all except NEWTON *and* SPENCER.

Spencer.   Sir John, what was the cause the king return'd so soon,
       And with such haste, so quickly to the shore?

Newton.   Bargeman, the king had reason for the same;
       I warrant thee he was not ill-advis'd.

[Handwritten margin note: is reassured they will not reason w him]

Sir John Newton: In Froissart's account of the Peasants' Revolt, it is Sir John Newton, not Morton, who is captured at Rochester and forced to act as the rebels' captain.

King: In the 1593 and 1604 printings, this line is not assigned to any character; however, based on the context, it is most likely meant for King Richard.

withal: With.

ordered: In addition to "commanded," may carry the sense of "returned to their proper place."

shrikes: Shrieks.

Make show: Act as though.

invade: Attack.

ungently: Rudely; roughly; inconsiderately.

entertain'd: Treated.

Spencer.   I think he meant to have commenced some talk with that
            unruly crew.

Newton.   'Twas thus: the king and all his company
            Being row'd with oars as far as Greenwich town,
            It was a world to see* what troupes of men,
            Like bees that swarm about the honey hive,
            Gan* strew the gravel ground and sandy plain
            That fill'd the air with cries and fearful noise
            And from the water did an echo rise
            That pierc'd the ears of our renowned king,
            Affrighting so his heart with strong conceit,
            Of some unhappy grievous stratagem*
            That, trust me, with my ears I hard him say
            He thought they would have all, like spaniels,*
            Ta'en water* desp'ratly and boarded him.
            So did they all yfare* like frantic men
            That time he thought to speed away apace
            And take the best advantage of the place.

Spencer.   Indeed, I could not greatly blame his Majesty;
            Myself was not so scar'd this seven year.
            Methought there was sufficient mouths enough
            At highest tide to have drawn the Thames dry.

---

a world to see: A wonder; incredible

Gan: Did.

conceit: Idea, belief.

grievous stratagem: Dangerous trick.

like spaniels: "Water spaniels" were trained by hunters to jump into water
    and swim to retrieve waterfowl that had been shot.

Ta'en water: Jumped into the water.

yfare: Behave.

Newton.   Spencer, ere it flow thrice* at London Bridge,
London, I fear, will hear a worser news.

Exit all.

---

ere it flow thrice: Before the tide flows three times. Newton is predicting a disaster will happen within three high tides at London Bridge, about 36 hours.

Scene 4

Enter JACK SHAW, WAT TYLER, HOB CARTER, TOM MILLER, NC MORTON, *and* SOUTHWARKMEN.

A Southwarkman.* Neighbors, you that keep the gates, let the king's liege
        people in, or we must be fain to* aid them with balls of wild
        fire* or some other device, for they have spoiled all Southwark,
        let out all the prisoners, broke up the Marshalsea and the
        King's Bench,* and made great havoc in the borough here.
        Therefore, I pray you, let them in.

Tyler.   Porter, open the gate; if thou lovest thyself, or thine own life,
        open the gate.

Miller.   You have a certain spare goose came in to be roasted. She is
        enough by this.

Exit all but MORTON.

Morton.   What mean these wretched miscreants,
        To make a spoil of* their own countrymen?
        Unnatural rebels! Whatsoe'er*
        By foreign foes may seem no whit so strange,

A Southwarkman: The text assigns this line to "Southwarkmen," but it was
    presumably intended to be spoken by a single representative of the
    inhabitants of the then-independent borough of Southwark.

be fain to: Be satisfied with; resort to.

balls of wild fire: Flammable material used as a weapon against an enemy
    fortification.

the Marshalsea and the King's Bench: Two prisons then located in
    Southwark.

make a spoil of: Plunder; pillage.

Whatsoe'er: Anything; Morton is saying that anything foreign foes may do
    will seem less strange than this domestic trouble. The scansion and the
    meaning suggest that part of this line may be missing.

As Englishmen to trouble England thus.
Well may I term it incest to the land,
Like foul lawless force and violence
Which Cinyras* did offer to his child.
O happy time, from all such troubles free!
What now, alas, is like to be the end of this attempt,
But that so long as they are glutted all with blood, they bathe
        therein?

Exit MORTON.

Cinyras: In Ovid's *Metamorphoses,* Myrrha tricked her father, Cinyras, king of
    Crete, into having sex with her. As punishment, Myrrha was transformed
    into the myrrh tree; the tree then bore the incestuous child, Adonis.

Scene 5

Enter NOBS *with a* FLEMING.*

Nobs. Sirrah, here it is set down by our captains that as many of you
as cannot say "bread and cheese" in good and perfect English,
ye die for it, and that was the cause so many strangers* did die
in Smithfield.* Let me hear you say "bread and cheese."

Fleming. Brock and keyse.

They exit.

[handwritten: How does he represent the rebellion]

[handwritten: ○ London welcomed foreigners for trades]

---

a Fleming: An immigrant from Flanders; many Flemish weavers were
working in London and throughout Europe at the time. This short scene
may be taken from Froissart, who reports that the rebels went from
street to street, killing all the Flemings they found.

strangers: Foreigners; immigrants.

Smithfield: Smithfield was used as a central meeting place for the rebels.

Fleming: In the original, no indication appears as to the speakers of these
lines. However, it seems clear from context that all but the last line is
spoken by Nobs, and the last line, in broken English, by the Fleming,
who is then presumably led off to be killed.

ACT THREE

Scene 1

Enter the KING, *the* LORD MAYOR, SIR JOHN NEWTON, *and two sergeants, with guards and gentlemen.*

King. Sir Newton, and Lord Mayor, this wrong that I am offered,
This open and unnatural injury:
A king to be thus hardly handled,
Of his own people and no other foes,
But such as have been brought up and bred in his own bosom,
Nourished with his tender care;
To be thus robbed of honour and of friends,
Thus daunted with continual frights and fears,
Haled* on to what mishap I cannot tell—
More hard mishap than had of like been mine,
Had I not marked* been to be a king.

Mayor. It shall become your Grace, most gracious lord,
To bear the mind in this afflicted time,
As other kings and lords hath done before,
Armed with sufferance* and magnanimity,
The one to make you resolute for chance*
The other forward* in your resolution.
The greatest wrong this rout hath done your grace,
Amongst a many wicked parts—

---

haled: Forced; pulled.

marked: Chosen.

sufferance: Patient endurance.

resolute for chance: Firm in the face of events.

forward: Spirited.

As in* frighting your worthy Lady Mother;
Making foul slaughter of your noblemen;
Burning up books and matters of records;
Defacing* houses of hostility,*
Saint John's* in Smithfield, the Savoy* and such like;
And beating down like wolves the better sort—
The greatest wrong in my opinion is
That in honour doth your person touch:
I mean they call your majesty to parley
And overbear you with a multitude,
As if you were a vassal, not a king.
O wretched minds of vile and barbarous men,
For whom the heavens have secret wreak* in store!
But, my Lord, with reverence and with pardon too,
Why comes your Grace into Smithfield near the crew
Unarm'd and guarded with so small a train?*

King.   If clemency may win their raging minds
To civil order, I'll approve it first.

As in...: The original printing has "Is in...," which appears to be a misprint. The items listed constitute a list of the "many wicked parts" before the Mayor returns to the "greatest wrong" later in this line.

Defacing: Damaging.

of hostility: The most likely reading is "because of their hostility;" that is, that the mob attack houses based on their ill-will towards the inhabitants.

Saint John's: The Priory of Order of St. John of Jerusalem, later known as the Knights Hospitaller. Robert Hales, the Lord Treasurer, was the prior of this order and was one of the men most hated by the mob; the priory and hospital were burned on June 13, 1381.

Savoy: Palace of John of Gaunt, burned to the ground and destroyed absolutely by the rebels on June 13, 1381, the day they entered into London. The Savoy was one of the richest and most ostentatious private buildings in London and was a symbol of the Duke of Lancaster's power and influence.

wreak: Retribution; punishment.

train: Escort.

They shall perceive me come in quiet wise,*
Accompanied with the Lord Mayor here alone,
Besides our guard that doth attend on us.

Mayor.   May it please your Grace that I shall raise the streets,*
To guard your Majesty through Smithfield as you walk?

King.   No, Lord Mayor, 'twill make them more outrageous,
And be a means to shed a world of blood:
I more account the blood of Englishmen than so.
But this is the place I have appointed them,
To hear them speak, and have adventured,
To come among this foul unruly crew:
And lo, my Lords, see where the people comes.

meeting

Enter JACK STRAW, WAT TYLER, TOM MILLER,* PARSON
BALL, *and* HOB CARTER.

Straw.   My masters, this is the king, come away,
'Tis he that would speak withal.

King.   Newton, desire that one may speak for all,
To tell the sum of their demand at full.

Newton.   My masters, you that are the special men,*
His Majesty requires you all by me,
That one may speak and tell him your demand,
And gently* here he lets you know by me,

---

wise: Manner.

raise the streets: Gather volunteers from the street.

Tom Miller: Again, it is not clear that Miller is really intended to enter here.
He does not speak until the next scene, which is preceded in the text by
"Exeunt Omnes" and "Enter Tom Miller;" in that scene, Nobs (who
does speak in this scene) tells Miller that he has been to Smithfield with
the captains. Most likely Miller's inclusion is a printer's error.

special men: Captains or officers.

gently: Courteously; the word also carries the sense of nobility of birth,
reminding the rebels of the king's royalty.

34

He is resolv'd to hear him all at large.*

King.	Aye, my good friends, I pray you heartily,
	Tell us your minds as mildly as you can;
	And we will answer you so well to all,
	As you shall not mislike* in any thing.

Straw.	We come to revenge your Officer's ill demands,
	And though we have kill'd him for his knavery,*
	Now we be gotten together, we will have wealth and liberty.

All.	Wealth and liberty!

King.	It is enough, believe me if you will,
	For as I am your true succeding prince,
	I swear by all the honour of my crown,
	You shall have liberty and pardon all,
	As God hath given it and your lawful king.

Tyler.	Ere we'll be pinch'd with poverty,
	To dig our meat and vittles* from the ground,
	That are as worthy of good maintenance,*
	As any gentleman your Grace doth keep,
	We will be kings and lords within ourselves,
	And not abide the pride of tyranny.

King.	I pray thee, fellow, what countryman art thou?

Tyler.	It skills* not much. I am an Englishman.

---

all at large: Everyone; in full.

mislike: Be displeased.

knavery: Misconduct.

meat and vittles: Food.

maintenance: Financial support or upkeep.

skills: Matters.

Ball.	Marry, sir, he is a Kentishman, and hath been my scholar* ere now.
Mayor.	Little good manners hath the villain learn'd To use his lord and king so barbarously.
King.	Well, people, ask you any more Than to be free and have your liberty?
All.	Wealth and liberty!
King.	Then take my word I promise to you all And eke* my general pardon now forthwith, Under my seal and letters patents to perform the same. Let every man betake him to his home, And with what speed our clerks* can make dispatch,* Your pardons and your letters patents* Shall be forthwith sent down in every shire.
Carter.	Marry, I thank your Grace, Hob Carter and the Essex men will home again, and we will take your word.
King.	We believe you all, and thank you all, And presently we will commandment* give, That all this business may be quickly ready.

Exit the KING *and his train.*

Straw.	I tell thee, Wat, this is not that I would have.

---

scholar: Student.

eke: Also.

clerks: Functionaries responsible for written work.

make dispatch: A double meaning; to act quickly and to prepare an official message.

letters patents: Royal decrees.

commandment: Orders.

I come for more than to be answered thus,
And if the Essex men will needs be gone,
Content, let them go suck their mams* at home—
I came for spoil, and spoil I'll have.

Tyler. Do what thou wilt, Jack; I will follow thee.

Nobs. How an if* it be to the gallows?

Tyler. Why, that is the worst.

Nobs. And in faith that is sure. But if you will be ruled by me,
Trust not to his pardon, for you die every mother's son,
But, captains, go forward as we have begun.

Ball. My masters, the boy speaks wisely.
I have read this in Cato: "ad cumsilium antiquam Voceris,"*
Take good counsel while it is given.

Straw. Content, boy, we will be ruled by thee.

*All exit.**

He is not
satisfied

---

suck their mams: Nurse at their mothers' breasts.

How an if: What if.

ad cumsilium antiquam Voceris: A misquotation from Cato. The original proverb, 'Ad consilium ne accesseris, antequam voceris' literally means 'do not come to the council chamber until you are called,' and figuratively 'do not speak until you are spoken to.'

All exit: The text at this point states 'Exeunt Omnes.' However, the next scene begins with a line by Nobs, but no direction for his entrance, although there is a direction for Miller's entrance at the beginning of the scene. Based on the dialogue, the following scene is intended to take place away from Smithfield. The most plausible staging is for Nobs to exit with the others and for Miller to enter and occupy some time in burning papers and other stage business before he is discovered by Nobs, as indicated below.

Scene 2

Enter TOM MILLER *to burn papers;* NOBS *enters and discovers him.*

Nobs.   Why, how now, Captain Miller, I perceive you take no care
which way the world goes.

Miller.   I'faith, Nobs, I have made a bonfire here of a great many
bonds and indentures and obligations,* faith I have been
amongst the ends of the court,* and among the records, and all
that I saw either in Guildhall* or in any other place, I have set
fire on them. But where hast thou been?

Nobs.   I have been with our captains, Straw and Tyler, at Saint John's
in Smithfield, but sirrah: I can tell you news, Captain Carter is
gone home, and all your Essex men, and I fear we shall be
hanged, therefore look you to yourself, for I will look to
myself.

Exit NOBS.

Miller.   Well, if we shall be hang'd, it is but a folly to be sorry,
But go to it with a good stomach,*
Riddle me riddle,* what this,
I shall be hang'd, I shall not be hang'd.

---

bonds and indentures and obligations: Documents evidencing loans and
debts.

the ends of the court: The Inns of Court, the portion of the City of London
where lawyers lived and practiced.

Guildhall: Guildhall, a stone building still standing in London, was at the time
the play was written the most important center of London law and
government.

with a good stomach: Boldly; with an appetite.

Riddle me riddle...: A conventional phrase used before asking a riddle; in this
case, the riddle or conundrum is whether Miller will be hanged or not.

*He tries** with a staff. Enter the* QUEEN MOTHER *and a* GENTLEMAN USHER.

Queen Mother. What doth that fellow?

Usher.   It seemeth, Madam, he disputeth with himself,
Whether he shall be hang'd or no.

Queen Mother. Alas, poor soul! Simple enough, God wot,*
And yet not so simple as a great many of his company.

Usher.   If it be as we are led to understand,
My lord the king hath given them general pardon.

Queen Mother. So he hath, and they like honest men are gone homewards,
or at the least the most part of them, but worse in my opinion
is their haps* that tarry longest.

Miller.   But peace, here is the king's mother. She can do much with the
king; I'll treat* her to beg my pardon of the king wisely:* I'll go
to her, humbly unto your worships, a poor Captain Thomas
Miller, requesting your favourable bequest, touching the
permission or destray,* towards the said Captain Miller, which
in blunt and flat terms is nominated, Sursum cordum, alis
dictus hangum meum,* from which place of torment God us

[handwritten annotation: Those who stay have worst outcomes]

---

tries: Tests; pretends (presumably to hang himself).

wot: Knows.

haps: Luck; fortune.

treat: Entreat; beseech.

wisely: Thusly.

destray: The meaning of this word is unclear.

Sursum cordum, alis dictus hangum meum: Quasi-Latin doggerel. "Sursum corda" is a line from the Latin mass that would have been familiar to the audience; literally, it means "lift up your hearts," but here is apparently meant to suggest a "cord;" with "hangum meum" it devolves into simply Latinate English.

all deliver and grant us to be merciful while we live here
together: Now sir, understanding your worship is the king's
mother, lamentably in the behalf before spoken, to stand
between me and the Gallows or to beg my pardon, in which
you shall not only save a proper handsome tall fellow and a
stout captain, but also you shall purchase all the prayers of all
the alewives in the town for saving a maltworm* and a
customer to help away their strong ale.

Queen Mother. What means the fellow by all this eloquence?

Usher.   It seems he fears he shall be hang'd,
             And therefore craves your Grace's favour in his behalf.

Queen Mother. Alas, poor fellow, he seemeth to be a stark nidiot.*
             Good fellow, if thou wilt go beg thy pardon of the king,
             I will speak for thee.

Miller.   Will you, in faith, and I will give you a tawdry lace.*

Usher.   Madam, here comes an unruly crew; let's begone.

             Exit QUEEN MOTHER and GENTLEMAN USHER;
             enter JACK STRAW, WAT TYLER, PARSON BALL,
             and NOBS to TOM MILLER.

Straw.   The king and his nobles think they may sleep in quiet,
             Now they have given us a little holy water at the court.
             But there's no such matter; we be no such fools,

---

maltworm: Drunkard; heavy drinker of beer.

nidiot: Idiot; simpleton.

tawdry lace: Contraction of "St. Audrey's lace," lace necklaces sold at the
    feast day of St. Ethelreda or Audrey, especially at Ely, were known as
    "tawdry." The modern meaning comes from the fact that they were
    often of low quality.

	To be bob'd out* with words and after come to hanging.
	Wat, do the thing thou comest for:
	If thou wilt be rul'd by me, we'll not leave it so.

Tyler. Ran tara,* have at all, my boys.

Miller. Sayest thou so, my heart? Then farewell my pardon,
For I'll do as ye do, hang together for company.

Ball. Neighbors and friends, never yield,
But fight it lustily in the field.
For God will give you strength and might
And put your enemies to flight;
To stand against them, day and night,
For of mine honesty your quarrel's right.

Miller. O Parson Ball, before you all,
If all fall out not well,
By following thy counsel,
And that by list'ning to thy talk
To the gallows we do walk:
Parson Ball, I will tell thee,
And swear it of my honesty,
Thou shalt be hang'd as well as we.

Straw. Peace; here comes the King, I trow.

Enter the KING, *the* LORD MAYOR,
and SIR JOHN NEWTON, *bearing a sword.*

King. What company be those, Newton, we do see;
Be them of those that promised us to part?*

---

bob'd out: Curtseyed to as we depart; Straw is saying that the king and the court would be polite as the rebels dispersed, but afterwards hunt them down and hang them, as did actually occur after the Peasants' Revolt.

Ran tara: Onomatopoeia imitating a trumpet.

part: Depart.

Newton.	Even part of those, my good and gracious lord,
	That promised your highness to depart.
King.	Why then, I see they stand not to their words.
	And sure they should not break it so with me,
	That have carefully remembred* them.
	This is a part of great ingratitude.
Mayor.	An it like* your Majesty, the Essex men
	With far more better minds have parted company,
	And every man beta'en him to his home.
	The chiefest of these rebels be of Kent,
	Of base degree and worse conditions* all,
	And vow'd,* as I am given to understand,
	To nothing but to havoc and to spoil.*
King.	Lord Mayor, if it be so, I wot*
	It is a dangerous and unnatural resolution.
	I pray thee, Newton, go and speak with them;
	Ask them what more it is that they require.
Newton.	My masters, you that be the chiefest of the rout,
	The king entreats you kindly here by me,
	To come and speak with him a word or two.
Straw.	Sirrah, if the king would anything with us,
	Tell him the way is indifferent to meet us.*

---

remembred: Given thought to; taken care of.

An it like: If it please.

base degree and worse conditions: Poor social rank, community status, and personal character.

vow'd: Committed; dedicated.

havoc...spoil: Plunder.

wot: Think; believe; understand.

the way is indifferent to meet us: It is as easy for him to come to us as for us to go to him.

| *Newton.* | You are too many to be talk'd with all. |
| | Besides, you owe a duty to your prince. |

| *Straw.* | Sirrah, give me the sword thou wearest there. |
| | Becomes it thee to be arm'd in my presence? |

| *Newton.* | Sir, I wear my weapon for mine own defence, |
| | And by your leave will wear it yet a while. |

| *Straw.* | What wilt thou, villain? Give it me, I say. |

| *King.* | Newton, give it him if that be all the matter. |
| | Here, take it and much good do it thee. |

The KING *gives him the sword.*

| *Straw.* | Villain, I say, give me the sword thou bearest up,* |
| | For that's the thing I tell thee I affect.* |

Newton.	This sword belongs unto my lord the king;
	'Tis none of mine, nor shalt thou have the same.
	Proud rebel, were but thou and I alone,
	Thou durst not ask it thus boldly, at my hands,
	For all the wealth this Smithfield doth contain.

| *Straw.* | By him that died for me, I will not dine |
| | Till I have seen thee hang'd or made away.* |

| *King.* | Alas, Lord Mayor, Newton is in great danger, |
| | And force cannot prevail against the rout. |

| *Mayor.* | Old Rome, I can remember I have read, |

---

give me the sword thou bearest up: In Froissart's telling, this exchange takes place between Wat Tyler and Richard's page. Tyler first asks the page for his own dagger, then for the sword he is carrying (here "bearing up") for the king.

affect: Want; desire.

made away: Killed.

When thou didst flourish for virtue, and for arms,
What magnanimity* did abide in thee:
Then, Walworth,* as it may become thee well,*
Deserve some honour at thy prince's hand,
And beautify this dignity of thine
With some or other act of consequence.
Villain, I say, whence comes this rage of thine?
How darest thou, a dunghill bastard born,
To brave* thy sovereign and his nobles thus?
Villain, I do arrest thee in my prince's name.
Proud rebel as thou art, take that withal,

Here he stabs him.

STRAW
IS
MURDERED

Learn thou, and all posterity after thee,
What 'tis a servile slave to brave a king.
Pardon, my gracious lord, for this, my fact,*
Is service done to God, and to yourself.

King.   Lord Mayor, for thy valiant act in this,
And noble courage in the king's behalf,
Thou shalt perceive us not to be ungrateful.

All.   Our captain is slain! Our captain is slain!

King.   Fear you not, people: I am your king,
And I will be your captain and your friend.

Newton.   Pleaseth your grace for to withdraw yourself,
These rebels then will soon be put to foil.*

---

magnanimity: Greatness of thought; noble character.

Walworth: This is the first time in the play the name of William Walworth, the Lord Mayor of London, is used.

as it may become thee well: In order to distinguish yourself.

brave: Defy.

fact: Deed, feat.

put to foil: Defeated; vanquished.

Mayor.   Soldiers, take heart to you and follow me!
It is our God that gives the victory.
Drag this accursed villain through the streets
To strike a terror to the rebels' hearts.
London will give you power and arms,
And God will strengthen you and daunt* your foes:
Fill Smithfield full of noise and joyful cries,
And say aloud, "God save our noble prince."

------

daunt: Intimidate.

ACT FOUR

Scene 1

Enter the KING, *the* LORD MAYOR, SIR JOHN MORTON, SIR JOHN NEWTON, *and* NOBLEMEN.

King. Lord Mayor, and well beloved friends,
Whose readiness in aid of us and ours
Hath given sure trial of your loyalty
And love you bear to us and to our land,
Sith,* by the help and mighty hand of God,
These foul unnatural broils* are quieted
And this unhappy tumult well appeas'd:*
Having, as law and duty binds us to,
Given both due praise and sacrifice, of thanks
Unto our God from whom this goodness comes,
Let me now to your counsel* recommend,
And to your sad opinions* generally,
This mighty business that we have in hand;
And that I may in brief unfold my mind:
My Lords, I would not yet, but mercy should
Against the law in this hard case prevail,
And, as I gave my word unto you all,
That if they then had left their mutiny,
Or rather had let fall their wrongful arms,*

Sith: Since.

broils: Disturbances; brawls.

appeas'd: Calmed; made quiet.

to your counsel: For your discussion.

sad opinions: Serious judgment.

arms: Weapons.

46

Their pardon then should have been general*—
So will I not, yet God forbid I should
(Though law I know exact* it at my hands)
Behold so many of my countrymen,
All done to death and strangled* in one day.
The end is this, that of that careless* rout
That hath so far unnaturally rebell'd,
The chief offenders may be punished.
And thus you know my mind, and so, my lords, proceed,
I pray you, and no other wise.*

Newton.   Sith* mercy in a prince resembleth right*
The gladsome* sunshine in a winter's day,
Pleaseth your Grace to pardon me to speak.*
When all the hope of life and breathing here
Be ta'en from all this rout in general,*
If then at instant of the dying hour
Your Grace's honourable person come,
To men half dead, kill'd wholly in conceit,*
Then, think I, it will be more gracious*
Than if it offered were so hastily;

---

general: Universal; complete.

exact: Demand; require.

strangled: Hanged.

careless: Unafraid; free from worry.

no other wise: Not in any other way.

Sith: Since.

right: Exactly; extremely.

gladsome: Pleasant; cheering.

Pleaseth your Grace to pardon me to speak: Please allow me to speak.

in general: All of them; all together.

kill'd wholly in conceit: Already thinking themselves dead.

gracious: Benevolent; pleasing.

When thread of life is almost fret in twain,
To give it strength breeds thanks and wonders too.

Mayor.   So many as are ta'en within the city
          Are fast in hold* to know your Grace's will.

King.   There is but one or two in all the rout
          Whom we would have to die for this offence;
          Especially* that by name are noted men:
          One is a naughty* and seditious priest;
          They call him Ball, as we are let to know,
          A person more notorious* than the rest,
          But this I do refer to your dispose.*

Newton.   Pleaseth your Grace, they have been rid apace,*
          Such special men* as we could possibly find,
          And many of the common rout among:
          And yet survives this Ball, that cursed priest,
          And one Wat Tyler, leader of the rest,
          Whose villanies and outrageous cruelties
          Have been so barbarously executed:*
          The one with malice of his traitorous taunts,
          The other with the violence of his hands,
          That gentle ruth* nor mercy hath no ears
          To hear them speak, much less to pardon them.

---

fast in hold: Held securely.

Especially: Specifically; in particular.

naughty: Wicked.

notorious: Infamous.

dispose: Arrangement; provision.

rid apace: Quickly and easily killed or defeated.

special men: Captains or officers.

executed: Performed.

ruth: Mercy; compassion.

King.   It is enough, I understand your minds.
           And well I wot,* in cases such as these,
           Kings may be found too full of clemency.
           But who are those that enter in this place?

Newton. Pleaseth it your Grace, these be the men
           Whom law hath worthily* condemn'd to die,
           Going to the place of execution.
           The foremost is that Ball, and next to him
           Wat Tyler, obstinate rebels both;
           For all the rest are of a better mold,
           Whose minds are softer than the famous* twain;
           For being common* soldiers in the camp,
           Were rather led with counsel of the rest,
           Deserving better to be pitied.

King.   Morton, to those condemned we see,
           Deliver this a pardon to them all,
           Excepting namely* those two foremost men:
           I mean the priest and him they call Wat Tyler.
           To all the rest free pardon we do send,
           And give the same to understand from us.

---

wot: Understand.

worthily: Deservedly.

famous: Notorious.

common: Low-ranking.

namely: Precisely; in particular.

The King's Pardon*

delivered by Sir John Morton to the Rebels

My friends and unhappy countrymen, whom the laws of England have worthily* condemned unto death for your open and unnatural rebellion against your lawful sovereign and anointed prince. I am sent unto you from the king's most excellent majesty to give you to understand, that notwithstanding this violence which you have offered to yourselves, in running furiously into the danger of the law, as mad and frantic men upon an eager sword, yet notwithstanding I say, that you have gathered rods to scourge your own selves,* following desperately your lewd* and ungovernable heads, which have haled* you on to this wretched and shameful end which is now so imminent over you all, that must in strangling cords die like dogs, and finish your lives in this miserable reproachful sort, because you would not live like men:

But far unlike yourselves, unlike Englishmen, degenerate from your natural obedience, and nature of your country, that by kind bringeth forth none such, or at least brooketh* none such, but spits them out for bastards and recreants:*

Notwithstanding, I say, this torment, wherein you now live looking every hour to suffer such a shameful and most detestable

---

The King's Pardon: In both the 1593 and 1604 printings, this speech is presented on a new page, with the heading "The King's Pardon delivered by Sir John Morton to the Rebels."

worthily: Deservedly.

gathered rods to scourge your own selves: To be beaten or whipped with your own rod was a common metaphor for self-sabotage or self-destructive behavior.

lewd: Ignorant, stupid or misguided.

haled: Dragged or pulled.

brooketh: Tolerates.

recreants: Cowards; shirkers of duty.

death; as doth commonly belong to such horrible offenders; yet it hath pleased the king of his accustomed goodness to give you your lives, and freely to forgive your faults, sending by me general pardon to you all, excepting one only accursed and seditious priest, that so far swerved from* the truth, and his allegience to his prince; and one Wat Tyler, whose outrage have been noted so outrageous in all his actions as for example to all Englishmen hereafter, his majesty hath thought good to account him and this parson, first stirrers in this tumult, and unnatural rebelling, the greatest offenders that now live to grieve his Majesty: and thus I have delivered the message of the king, which is in effect, general pardon to you all, and a sentence of death unto the archrebels, John Ball, and Wat Tyler:

For which great grace, if you think yourselves any thing bound to his highness, as infinitely you are, let it appear as far forth hereafter as you may, either by outward figures of duty, or inward loyalty of hearts expressed, and to begin the same, in sign of your thankfulness, say all, "God save the king!"

All.   God save the king!

Tyler.   Well, then, we know the worst.
            He can but hang us, and that is all,
            Were Jack Straw alive again,
            And I in as good possibility* as ever I was,
            I would lay a surer trump,*
            Ere I would lose so fair a trick.

Ball.   And what I said in time of our business I repent not,
            And if it were* to speak again,
            Every word should be a sermon.
            So much I do repent me.

---

swerved from: Forsook; turned away from.

possibility: Circumstances.

lay a surer trump: In other words, given another chance, Tyler would try harder to achieve his goals, rather than giving them up.

if it were: If I were able.

Morton.	Away with the rebels, suffer them not to speak;
	His words are poison in the ears of the people.
	Away, villain, stain to thy country and thy calling.
Tyler.	Why, Morton, are you so lusty with a pox?*
	I pull'd you out of Rochester casle by the poll.*
Morton.	And in recompence I will help to set your head on a pole.
Tyler.	Pray you, let's be poll'd* first.
Morton.	Away with the rebels.

Exit the rebels.

Morton.	As gave your Grace in charge,* I have delivered
	Your Highness' pleasure amongst the prisoners,
	And have proclaim'd your Grace's pardon amongst them all,
	Save only those two unnatural Englishmen,
	O might I say no English nor men,
	That Ball and Tyler, cursed rebels both,
	Whom I commanded to be executed:
	And in you Highness' name have freed all the rest,
	Whose thankful hearts I find as full replete,*
	With signs of joy and duty to your Grace,
	As those unnatural rebels' hateful mouths
	Are full of foul speeches, and unhonourable.

---

so lusty with a pox: So cheerful or energetic despite your disease. The pox might refer to a visible skin disease but here, used as an insult, more likely means syphilis.

poll: Hair.

let's be poll'd: Let's put it to a vote.

As gave your Grace in charge: As your Grace ordered me to do.

full replete: Abundantly full; full to bursting.

52

King.　　　　It is no matter, Morton, let them bark;
　　　　　　I trow* they cannot bite when they be dead.
　　　　　　And Lord Mayor, for your valiant act
　　　　　　And dangerous attempt, in our behalf,
　　　　　　To free your country and your king from ill:
　　　　　　In our behalf and in our common weal,*
　　　　　　We will accept it as the deed deserves,
　　　　　　And thank you for this honourable attempt.

Mayor.　　　What subjects' hearts could brook* the rage of theirs,
　　　　　　To vaunt* in presence of their sovereign lord,
　　　　　　To brave* him to his face before his peers,
　　　　　　But would by policy or force attempt
　　　　　　To quell the raging of such furious foes?
　　　　　　My sovereign lord, 'twas but my duty done,
　　　　　　First unto God, next to my lawful king,
　　　　　　Proceeding from a true and loyal heart,
　　　　　　And so I hope your Grace esteems thereof.

King.　　　　To the end this deed shall rest in memory,
　　　　　　Which shall continue forever to the end:
　　　　　　Lord Mayor, I'll adorn to thy degree
　　　　　　Another title of a lasting fame.
　　　　　　Kneel down, William Walworth, and receive
　　　　　　By mine own hand the order of knighthood:
　　　　　　Stand up Sir William, first knight of thy degree,
　　　　　　But henceforth all which should succeed thy place,
　　　　　　Shall have like honour for thy noble deed;

---

trow: Trust.

weal: Good; the welfare of the community.

brook: Tolerate; put up with.

vaunt: Boast.

brave: Defy.

Besides, that time shall ne'er abridge thy fame,
The city arms shall bear, for memory,
The bloody dagger, the more for Walworth's honour.
Call for your herald, and receive your due.

Mayor. My gracious lord, this honourable grace,
So far above desert, sith* what I did
My duty and allegiance bad me do,
Binds me and my successors evermore,
With sweet encouragement to the like attempt,
Your Majesty and all your royal peers
Shall find your London such a storehouse still,
As not alone you shall command our wealth,
But loyal hearts, the treasure of a prince,
Shall grow like grains sown in a fertile soil.
And God I praise that with his holy hand
Hath given me heart to free my prince and land.

King. Then sith* these dangerous broils are over pass'd
With shedding of such little English blood,
'Tis for the fame and honour of a prince
Well to reward the actors of the same,
So many of thy bretheren as accompanied thee,
In Smithfield here about this bold attempt;
When time shall serve I'll knight them as thou art.
And so, Lord Mayor, Newton, Morton, and the rest,
Accompany us to guard us to the Tower,
Where we'll repose and rest ourselves all night.

---

sith: Since.

54

Appendix

This appendix contains materials related to the play but not likely to be of primary interest to the casual reader. In this case, this includes a brief account of John Ball's sermon at Blackheath, from Walsingham's Chronicle, and accounts of the Peasants' Revolt from Froissart's *Chronicle* and from Charles Dickens' *Child's History of England*.

Walsingham's Account of
John Ball's Sermon at Blackheath

The primary account of John Ball's sermon at Blackheath, containing the famous lines quoted in Act 1 Scene 1, is from Thomas Walsingham's Historia Anglicana, *in which all but the famous rhyming tag are given in Latin. The translation below is by English historian John Stow (1525-1605) and may have been familiar to the author of Jack Straw.*

That his doctrines might infect the more numbers of people, at Blackheath, where they were many thousands of the commons assembled, he began his sermon in this manner:—

> When Adam delved and Eve span,
> Who was then a gentleman?

And, continuing his begun sermon, he sought by the word of that proverb, which he took for his theme, to introduce and prove, that from the beginning all were made alike by nature, and that bondage or servitude was brought in by unjust oppression of naughty men against the will of God; for if it had pleased God to have made bondmen, he would have appointed them from the beginning of the world, who should have been slave and who lord. They ought to consider, therefore, that now there was a time given them by God, in the which, laying aside the yoke of continual bondage, they might, if they would, enjoy their long wished-for liberty. Wherefore he admonished them, that they should be wise, and after the manner of a good husbandman that tilled his ground, and did cut away all noisome weeds that were accustomed to grow and oppress the fruit, that they should make haste to do now at this present the like. First, the archbishop and great men of the kingdom were to be slain; after, lawyers, justiciars, and questmongers; lastly, whomsoever they knew likely hereafter to be hurtful to the commons, they should dispatch out of the land, for so might they purchase safety to themselves hereafter, if the great men being once taken away, there were among them equal liberty, all one nobility, and like dignity, one semblable authority or power. These and many such mad devices he preached, which made the common people to esteem of him in such manner, as they cried out, he should be the archbishop of Canterbury and chancellor of the realm, for he only deserved the honour.

Froissart's Account of the Peasants' Revolt of 1381

This English translation of Froissart's Chronicles *is that of John Bourchier (1467-1533), who translated the* Chronicles *at the request of King Henry VIII, as edited and in some places summarized by the great English historian George Macaulay, based on Macaulay's published edition of 1895. The description of the Revolt begins immediately after the discussion of unrelated treaty discussions between England and Scotland, here omitted. The "Duke of Lancaster" referred to in the text is John of Gaunt, who was involved in the Scottish negotiations and thus was not in London when hostilities broke out.*

How the earl of Cambridge departed out of England to go into Portugal; and how the commons of England rebelled against the noblemen.

...In the mean season while this treaty was, there fell in England great mischief and rebellion of moving of the common people, by which deed England was at a point to have been lost without recovery. There was never realm nor country in so great adventure as it was in that time, and all because of the ease and riches that the common people were of, which moved them to this rebellion, as sometime they did in France, the which did much hurt, for by such incidents the realm of France hath been greatly grieved.

It was a marvellous thing and of poor foundation that this mischief began in England, and to give ensample to all manner of people I will speak hereof as it was done, as I was informed, and of the incidents thereof. There was an usage in England, and yet is in divers countries, that the noblemen hath great franchise over the commons and keepeth them in servage, that is to say, their tenants ought by custom to labour the lords' lands, to gather and bring home their corns, and some to thresh and to fan, and by servage to make their hay and to hew their wood and bring it home. All these things they ought to do by servage, and there be more of these people in England than in any other realm. Thus the noblemen and prelates are served by them, and especially in the county of Kent, Essex, Sussex and Bedford. These unhappy people of these said countries began to stir, because they said they were kept in great servage, and in the beginning of the world, they said, there were no bondmen, wherefore they maintained that none ought to be bond, without he did treason to his lord, as Lucifer did to God; but they said they could have no such battle, for they were neither angels nor spirits, but men formed to the similitude of their lords, saying why should they then be kept so under like beasts; the which they said they would no longer suffer, for they would be all one, and if they laboured or did anything for their lords, they would have wages therefor as well as other. And of this imagination was a foolish priest in the country of Kent called John Ball, for the which foolish words he had been three times in the bishop of Canterbury's prison: for this priest used oftentimes on the Sundays after mass, when the people were going out of the minster, to go into the cloister and preach, and made the people to assemble about him, and would say thus: 'Ah, ye good people, the matters goeth not well to pass in England, nor shall not do till everything be common, and that there be no villains nor gentlemen, but that we may be all united together, and that the lords be no greater masters than we be. What have we deserved, or why should we be kept thus in servage? We be all come from one father and one mother, Adam and Eve: whereby can they say or shew that they be greater lords than we be, saving by that they cause us to win and labour for that they dispend? They are clothed in velvet and camlet furred with grise, and we be vestured with poor cloth: they have their wines, spices and good bread, and we have the drawing out of the chaff and drink water; they dwell in fair houses, and we have the pain and travail, rain and wind in the fields; and by that that cometh of our labours they keep and maintain their estates: we be called their bondmen, and without we do readily them service, we be beaten; and we have no sovereign to whom we may complain, nor that will hear us nor do us right. Let us go to the king, he is young, and shew him what servage we be in, and shew him how we will have it otherwise, or else we will provide us of some remedy; and if we go together, all manner of people that be now in any bondage will follow us to the intent to be made free; and when the king seeth us, we shall have some remedy, either by fairness or otherwise.' Thus John Ball said on Sundays, when the people issued out of the churches in the villages; wherefore many of the mean people loved him, and such as intended to no goodness said how he said truth; and so they would murmur one with another in the fields and in the ways as they went together, affirming how John Ball said truth.

The archbishop of Canterbury, who was informed of the saying of this John Ball, caused him to be taken and put in prison a two or three months to chastise him: howbeit, it had been much better at the beginning that he had been condemned to perpetual prison or else to have died, rather than to have suffered him to have been again delivered out of prison; but the bishop had conscience to let him die. And when this John Ball was out of prison, he returned again to his error, as he did before.

Of his words and deeds there were much people in London informed, such as had great envy at them that were rich and such as were noble; and then they began to speak among them and said how the realm of England was right evil governed, and how that gold and silver was taken from them by them that were named noblemen: so thus these unhappy men of London began to rebel and assembled them together, and sent word to the foresaid countries that they should come to London and bring their people with them, promising them how they should find London open to receive them and the commons of the city to be of the same accord, saying how they would do so much to the king that there should not be one bondman in all England.

This promise moved so them of Kent, of Essex, of Sussex, of Bedford and of the countries about, that they rose and came towards London to the number of sixty thousand. And they had a captain called Water Tyler, and with him in company was Jack Straw and John Ball: these three were chief sovereign captains, but the head of all was Water Tyler, and he was indeed a tiler of houses, an ungracious patron. When these unhappy men began thus to stir, they of London, except such as were of their band, were greatly affrayed. Then the mayor of London and the rich men of the city took counsel together, and when they saw the people thus coming on every side, they caused the gates of the city to be closed and would suffer no man to enter into the city. But when they had well imagined, they advised not so to do, for they thought they should thereby put their suburbs in great peril to be brent; and so they opened again the city, and there entered in at the gates in some place a hundred, two hundred, by twenty and by thirty, and so when they came to London, they entered and lodged: and yet of truth the third part of these people could not tell what to ask or demand, but followed each other like beasts, as the shepherds did of old time, saying how they would go conquer the Holy Land, and at last all came to nothing. In like wise these villains and poor people came to London, a hundred mile off, sixty mile, fifty mile, forty mile, and twenty mile off, and from all countries about London, but the most part came from the countries before named, and as they came they demanded ever for the king. The gentlemen of the countries, knights and squires, began to doubt, when they saw the people began to rebel; and though they were in doubt, it was good reason; for a less occasion they might have been affrayed. So the gentlemen drew together as well as they might.

The same day that these unhappy people of Kent were coming to London, there returned from Canterbury the king's mother, princess of Wales, coming from her pilgrimage. She was in great jeopardy to have been lost, for these people came to her chare and dealt rudely with her, whereof the good lady was in great doubt lest they would have done some villany to her or to her damosels. Howbeit, God kept her, and she came in one day from Canterbury to London, for she never durst tarry by the way. The same time king Richard her son was at the Tower of London: there his mother found him, and with him there was the earl of Salisbury, the archbishop of Canterbury, sir Robert of Namur, the lord of Gommegnies and divers other, who were in doubt of these people that thus gathered together, and wist not what they demanded. This rebellion was well known in the king's court, or any of these people began to stir out of their houses; but the king nor his council did provide no remedy therefor, which was great marvel. And to the intent that all lords and good people and such as would nothing but good should take ensample to correct them that be evil and rebellious, I shall shew you plainly all the matter, as it was.

The evil deeds that these commons of England
did to the king's officers, and how they sent a knight
to speak with the king.

The Monday before the feast of Corpus Christi the year of our Lord God a thousand three hundred and eighty-one these people issued out of their houses to come to London to speak with the king to be made free, for they would have had no bondman in England. And so first they came to Saint Thomas of Canterbury, and there John Ball had thought to have found the bishop of Canterbury, but he was at London with the king. When Wat Tyler and Jack Straw entered into Canterbury, all the common people made great feast, for all the town was of their assent; and there they took counsel to go to London to the king, and to send some of their company over the river of Thames into Essex, into Sussex and into the counties of Stafford and Bedford, to speak to the people that they should all come to the farther side of London and thereby to close London round about, so that the king should not stop their passages, and that they should all meet together on Corpus Christi day. They that were at Canterbury entered into Saint Thomas' church and did there much hurt, and robbed and brake up the bishop's chamber, and in robbing and bearing out their pillage they said: 'Ah, this chancellor of England hath had a good market to get together all this riches: he shall give us now account of the revenues of England and of the great profits that he hath gathered sith the king's coronation.' When they had this Monday thus broken the abbey of Saint Vincent, they departed in the morning and all the people of Canterbury with them, and so took the way to Rochester and sent their people to the villages about. And in their going they beat down and robbed houses of advocates and procurers of the king's court and of the archbishop, and had mercy of none. And when they were come to Rochester, they had there good cheer; for the people of that town tarried for them, for they were of the same sect, and then they went to the castle there and took the knight that had the rule thereof, he was called sir John Newton, and they said to him: 'Sir, it behoveth you to go with us and you shall be our sovereign captain and to do that we will have you.' The knight excused himself honestly and shewed them divers considerations and excuses, but all availed him nothing, for they said unto him: 'Sir John, if ye do not as we will have you, ye are but dead,' The knight, seeing these people in that fury and ready to slay him, he then doubted death and agreed to them, and so they took him with them against his inward will; and in like wise did they of other counties in England, as Essex, Sussex, Stafford, Bedford and Warwick, even to Lincoln; for they brought the knights and gentlemen into such obeisance, that they caused them to go with them, whether they would or not, as the lord Moylays, a great baron, sir Stephen of Hales and sir Thomas of Cosington and other.

Now behold the great fortune. If they might have come to their intents, they would have destroyed all the noblemen of England, and thereafter all other nations would have followed the same and have taken foot and ensample by them and by them of Gaunt and Flanders, who rebelled against their lord. The same year the Parisians rebelled in like wise and found out the mallets of iron, of whom there were more than twenty thousand, as ye shall hear after in this history; but first we will speak of them of England.

When these people thus lodged at Rochester departed, and passed the river and came to Brentford, alway keeping still their opinions, beating down before them and all about the places and houses of advocates and procurers, and striking off the heads of divers persons. And so long they went forward till they came within a four mile of London, and there lodged on a hill called Blackheath; and as they went, they said ever they were the king's men and the noble commons of England: and when they of London knew that they were come so near to them, the mayor, as ye have heard before, closed the gates and kept straitly all the passages. This order caused the mayor, who was called Nicholas Walworth, and divers other rich burgesses of the city, who were not of their sect; but there were in London of their unhappy opinions more than thirty thousand.

Then these people thus being lodged on Blackheath determined to send their knight to speak with the king and to shew him how all that they have done or will do is for him and his honour, and how the realm of England hath not been well governed a great space for the honour of the realm nor for the common profit by his uncles and by the clergy, and specially by the archbishop of Canterbury his chancellor; whereof they would have account. This knight durst do none otherwise, but so came by the river of Thames to the Tower. The king and they that were with him in the Tower, desiring to hear tidings, seeing this knight coming made him way, and was brought before the king into a chamber; and with the king was the princess his mother and his two brethren, the earl of Kent and the lord John Holland, the earl of Salisbury, the earl of Warwick, the earl of Oxford, the archbishop of Canterbury, the lord of Saint John's, sir Robert of Namur, the lord of Vertaing, the lord of Gommegnies, sir Henry of Senzeille, the mayor of London and divers other notable burgesses. This knight sir John Newton, who was well known among them, for he was one of the king's officers, he kneeled down before the king and said: 'My right redoubted lord, let it not displease your grace the message that I must needs shew you, for, dear sir, it is by force and against my will.' 'Sir John,' said the king, 'say what ye will: I hold you excused.' 'Sir, the commons of this your realm hath sent me to you to desire you to come and speak with them on Blackheath; for they desire to have none but you: and, sir, ye need not to have any doubt of your person, for they will do you no hurt; for they hold and will hold you for their king. But, sir, they say they will shew you divers things, the which shall be right necessary for you to take heed of, when they speak with you; of the which things, sir, I have no charge to shew you: but, sir, it may please you to give me an answer such as may appease them and that they may know for truth that I have spoken with you; for they have my children in hostage till I return again to them, and without I return again, they will slay my children incontinent.'

Then the king made him an answer and said: 'Sir, ye shall have an answer shortly.' Then the king took counsel what was best for him to do, and it was anon determined that the next morning the king should go down the river by water and without fail to speak with them. And when sir John Newton heard that answer, he desired nothing else and so took his leave of the king and of the lords and returned again into his vessel, and passed the Thames and went to Blackheath, where he had left more than threescore thousand men. And there he answered them that the next morning they should send some of their council to the Thames, and there the king would come and speak with them. This answer greatly pleased them, and so passed that night as well as they might, and the fourth part of them fasted for lack of victual for they had none, wherewith they were sore displeased, which was good reason.

All this season the earl of Buckingham was in Wales, for there he had fair heritages by reason of his wife, who was daughter to the earl of Northumberland and Hereford; but the voice was all through London how he was among these people. And some said certainly how they had seen him there among them; and all was because there was one Thomas in their company, a man of the county of Cambridge, that was very like the earl. Also the lords that lay at Plymouth to go into Portugal were well informed of this rebellion and of the people that thus began to rise; wherefore they doubted lest their viage should have been broken, or else they feared lest the commons about Hampton, Winchester and Arundel would have come on them: wherefore they weighed up their anchors and issued out of the haven with great pain, for the wind was sore against them, and so took the sea and there cast anchor abiding for the wind. And the duke of Lancaster, who was in the marches of Scotland between Moorlane and Roxburgh entreating with the Scots, where it was shewed him of the rebellion, whereof he was in doubt, for he knew well he was but little beloved with the commons of England;

howbeit, for all those tidings, yet he did sagely demean himself as touching the treaty with the Scots. The earl Douglas, the earl of Moray, the earl of Sutherland and the earl Thomas Versy, and the Scots that were there for the treaty knew right well the rebellion in England, how the common people in every part began to rebel against the noblemen; wherefore the Scots thought that England was in great danger to be lost, and therefore in their treaties they were the more stiffer against the duke of Lancaster and his council.

Now let us speak of the commons of England and how they persevered.

How the commons of England entered into London,
and of the great evil that they did,
and ofthe death of the Bishop of Canterbury
and divers other.

In the morning on Corpus Christi day king Richard heard mass in the Tower of London, and all his lords, and then he took his barge with the earl of Salisbury, the earl of Warwick, the earl of Oxford and certain knights, and so rowed down along the Thames to Rotherhithe, whereas was descended down the hill a ten thousand men to see the king and to speak with him. And when they saw the king's barge coming, they began to shout, and made such a cry, as though all the devils of hell had been among them. And they had brought with them sir John Newton to the intent that, if the king had not come, they would have stricken him all to pieces, and so they had promised him. And when the king and his lords saw the demeanour of the people, the best assured of them were in dread; and so the king was counselled by his barons not to take any landing there, but so rowed up and down the river. And the king demanded of them what they would, and said how he was come thither to speak with them, and they said all with one voice: 'We would that ye should come aland, and then we shall shew you what we lack.' Then the earl of Salisbury answered for the king and said: 'Sirs, ye be not in such order nor array that the king ought to speak with you.' And so with those words no more said: and then the king was counselled to return again to the Tower of London, and so he did.

And when these people saw that, they were inflamed with ire and returned to the hill where the great band was, and there shewed them what answer they had and how the king was returned to the Tower of London. Then they cried all with one voice, 'Let us go to London,' and so they took their way thither; and in their going they beat down abbeys and houses of advocates and of men of the court, and so came into the suburbs of London, which were great and fair, and there beat down divers fair houses, and specially they brake up the king's prisons, as the Marshalsea and other, and delivered out all the prisoners that were within: and there they did much hurt, and at the bridge foot they threat them of London because the gates of the bridge were closed, saying how they would bren all the suburbs and so conquer London by force, and to slay and bren all the commons of the city. There were many within the city of their accord, and so they drew together and said: 'Why do we not let these good people enter into the city? they are your fellows, and that that they do is for us.' So therewith the gates were opened, and then these people entered into the city and went into houses and sat down to eat and drink. They desired nothing but it was incontinent brought to them, for every man was ready to make them good cheer and to give them meat and drink to appease them.

Then the captains, as John Ball, Jack Straw and Wat Tyler, went throughout London and a twenty thousand with them, and so came to the Savoy in the way to Westminster, which was a goodly house and it pertained to the duke of Lancaster. And when they entered, they slew the keepers thereof and robbed and pilled the house, and when they had so done, then they set fire on it and clean destroyed and brent it. And when they had done that outrage, they left not therewith, but went straight to the fair hospital of the Rhodes called Saint John's, and there they brent house, hospital, minster and all. Then they went from street to street and slew all the Flemings that they could find in church or in any other place, there was none respited from death. And they brake up divers houses of the Lombards and robbed them and took their goods at their pleasure, for there was none that durst say them nay. And they slew in the city a rich merchant called Richard Lyon, to whom before that time Wat Tyler had done service in France; and on a time this Richard Lyon had beaten him, while he was his varlet, the which Wat Tyler then remembered and so came to his house and strake off his head and caused it to be borne on a spear-point before him all about the city. Thus these ungracious people demeaned themselves like people enraged and wood, and so that day they did much sorrow in London.

And so against night they went to lodge at Saint Katherine's before the Tower of London, saying how they would never depart thence till they had the king at their pleasure and till he had accorded to them all [they would ask, and] that they would ask accounts of the chancellor of England, to know where all the good was become that he had levied through the realm, and without he made a good account to them thereof, it should not be for his profit. And so when they had done all these evils to the strangers all the day, at night they lodged before the Tower.

Ye may well know and believe that it was great pity for the danger that the king and such as were with him were in. For some time these unhappy people shouted and cried so loud, as though all the devils of hell had been among them. In this evening the king was counselled by his brethren and lords and by sir Nicholas Walworth, mayor of London, and divers other notable and rich burgesses, that in the night time they should issue out of the Tower and enter into the city, and so to slay all these unhappy people, while they were at their rest and asleep; for it was thought that many of them were drunken, whereby they should be slain like flies; also of twenty of them there was scant one in harness. And surely the good men of London might well have done this at their ease, for they had in their houses secretly their friends and servants ready in harness, and also sir Robert Knolles was in his lodging keeping his treasure with a sixscore ready at his commandment; in like wise was sir Perducas d'Albret, who was as then in London, insomuch that there might well [have] assembled together an eight thousand men ready in harness. Howbeit, there was nothing done, for the residue of the commons of the city were sore doubted, lest they should rise also, and the commons before were a threescore thousand or more. Then the earl of Salisbury and the wise men about the king said: 'Sir, if ye can appease them with fairness, it were best and most profitable, and to grant them everything that they desire, for if we should begin a thing the which we could not achieve, we should never recover it again, but we and our heirs ever to be disinherited,' So this counsel was taken and the mayor countermanded, and so commanded that he should not stir; and he did as he was commanded, as reason was. And in the city with the mayor there were twelve aldermen, whereof nine of them held with the king and the other three took part with these ungracious people, as it was after well known, the which they full dearly bought.

And on the Friday in the morning the people, being at Saint Katharine's near to the Tower, began to apparel themselves and to cry and shout, and said, without the king would come out and speak with them, they would assail the Tower and take it by force, and slay all them that were within. Then the king doubted these words and so was counselled that he should issue out to speak with them: and then the king sent to them that they should all draw to a fair plain place called Mile-end, whereas the people of the city did sport them in the summer season, and there the king to grant them that they desired; and there it was cried in the king's name, that whosoever would speak with the king let him go to the said place, and there he should not fail to find the king. Then the people began to depart, specially the commons of the villages, and went to the same place: but all went not thither, for they were not all of one condition; for there were some that desired nothing but riches and the utter destruction of the noblemen and to have London robbed and pilled; that was the principal matter of their beginning, the which they well shewed, for as soon as the Tower gate opened and that the king was issued out with his two brethren and the earl of Salisbury, the earl of Warwick, the earl of Oxford, sir Robert of Namur, the lord of Vertaing, the lord Gommegnies and divers other, then Wat Tyler, Jack Straw and John Ball and more than four hundred entered into the Tower and brake up chamber after chamber, and at last found the archbishop of Canterbury, called Simon, a valiant man and a wise, and chief chancellor of England, and a little before he had said mass before the king. These gluttons took him and strake off his head, and also they beheaded the lord of Saint John's and a friar minor, master in medicine, pertaining to the duke of Lancaster, they slew him in despite of his master, and a sergeant at arms called John Leg; and these four heads were set on four long spears and they made them to be borne before them through the streets of London and at last set them a-high on London bridge, as though they had been traitors to the king and to the realm. Also these gluttons entered into the princess' chamber and brake her bed, whereby she was so sore affrayed that she swooned; and there she was taken up and borne to the water side and put into a barge and covered, and so conveyed to a place called the Queen's Wardrobe; and there she was all that day and night like a woman half dead, till she was comforted with the king her son, as ye shall hear after.

How the nobles of England were in great peril
to have been destroyed, and how these rebels were punished
and sent home to their own houses.

When the king came to the said place of Mile-end without London, he put out of his company his two brethren, the earl of Kent and sir John Holland, and the lord of Gommegnies, for they durst not appear before the people: and when the king and his other lords were there, he found there a threescore thousand men of divers villages and of sundry countries in England; so the king entered in among them and said to them sweetly: 'Ah, ye good people, I am your king: what lack ye? what will ye say?' Then such as understood him said: 'We will that ye make us free for ever, ourselves, our heirs and our lands, and that we be called no more bond nor so reputed.' 'Sirs,' said the king, 'I am well agreed thereto. Withdraw you home into your own houses and into such villages as ye came from, and leave behind you of every village two or three, and I shall cause writings to be made and seal them with my seal, the which they shall have with them, containing everything that ye demand; and to the intent that ye shall be the better assured, I shall cause my banners to be delivered into every bailiwick, shire and countries.'

These words appeased well the common people, such as were simple and good plain men, that were come thither and wist not why. They said, 'It was well said, we desire no better.' Thus these people began to be appeased and began to withdraw them into the city of London. And the king also said a word, the which greatly contented them. He said: 'Sirs, among you good men of Kent ye shall have one of my banners with you, and ye of Essex another, and ye of Sussex, of Bedford, of Cambridge, of Yarmouth, of Stafford and of Lynn, each of you one; and also I pardon everything that ye have done hitherto, so that ye follow my banners and return home to your houses.' They all answered how they would so do: thus these people departed and went into London. Then the king ordained more than thirty clerks the same Friday, to write with all diligence letter patents and sealed with the king's seal, and delivered them to these people; and when they had received the writing, they departed and returned into their own countries: but the great venom remained still behind, for Wat Tyler, Jack Straw and John Ball said, for all that these people were thus appeased, yet they would not depart so, and they had of their accord more than thirty thousand. So they abode still and made no press to have the king's writing nor seal, for all their intents was to put the city to trouble in such wise as to slay all the rich and honest persons and to rob and pill their houses. They of London were in great fear of this, wherefore they kept their houses privily with their friends and such servants as they had, every man according to his puissance. And when these said people were this Friday thus somewhat appeased, and that they should depart as soon as they had their writings, every man home into his own country, then king Richard came into the Royal, where the queen his mother was, right sore affrayed: so he comforted her as well as he could and tarried there with her all that night.

Yet I shall shew you of an adventure that fell by these ungracious people before the city of Norwich, by a captain among them called Guilliam Lister of Stafford. The same day of Corpus Christi that these people entered into London and brent the duke of Lancaster's house, called the Savoy; and the hospital of Saint John's and brake up the king's prisons and did all this hurt, as ye have heard before, the same time there assembled together they of Stafford, of Lynn, of Cambridge, of Bedford and of Yarmouth; and as they were coming towards London, they had a captain among them called Lister. And as they came, they rested them before Norwich, and in their coming they caused every man to rise with them, so that they left no villains behind them. The cause why they rested before Norwich I shall shew you. There was a knight, captain of the town, called sir Robert Sale. He was no gentleman born, but he had the grace to be reputed sage and valiant in arms, and for his valiantness king Edward made him knight. He was of his body one of the biggest knights in all England. Lister and his company thought to have had this knight with them and to make him their chief captain, to the intent to be the more feared and beloved: so they sent to him that he should come and speak with them in the field, or else they would bren the town. The knight considered that it was better for him to go and speak with them rather than they should do that outrage to the town: then he mounted on his horse and issued out of the town all alone, and so came to speak with them. And when they saw him, they made him great cheer and honoured him much, desiring him to alight off his horse and to speak with them, and so he did: wherein he did great folly; for when he was alighted, they came round about him and began to speak fair to him and said: 'Sir Robert, ye are a knight and a man greatly beloved in this country and renowned a valiant man; and though ye be thus, yet we know you well, ye be no gentleman born, but son to a villain such as we be. Therefore come you with us and be our master, and we shall make you so great a lord, that one quarter of England shall be under your obeisance,' When the knight heard them speak thus, it was greatly contrarious to his mind, for he thought never to make any such bargain, and answered them with a felonous regard: 'Fly away, ye ungracious people, false and evil traitors that ye be: would you that I should forsake my natural lord for such a company of knaves as ye be, to my dishonour for ever? I had rather ye were all hanged, as ye shall be; for that shall be your end.' And with those words he had thought to have leapt again upon his horse, but he failed of the stirrup and the horse started away. Then they cried all at him and said: 'Slay him without mercy.' When he heard those words, he let his horse go and drew out a good sword and began to scrimmish with them, and made a great place about him, that it was pleasure to behold him. There was none that durst approach near him: there were some that approached near him, but at every stroke that he gave he cut off other leg, head or arm: there was none so hardy but that they feared him: he did there such deeds of arms that it was marvel to regard. But there were more than forty thousand of these unhappy people: they shot and cast at him, and he was unarmed: to say truth, if he had been of iron or steel, yet he must needs have been slain; but yet, or he died, he slew twelve out of hand, beside them that he hurt. Finally he was stricken to the earth, and they cut off his arms and legs and then strake his body all to pieces. This was the end of sir Robert Sale, which was great damage; for which deed afterward all the knights and squires of England were angry and sore displeased when they heard thereof.

Now let us return to the king. The Saturday the king departed from the Wardrobe in the Royal and went to Westminster and heard mass in the church there, and all his lords with him. And beside the church there was a little chapel with an image of our Lady, which did great miracles and in whom the kings of England had ever great trust and confidence. The king made his orisons before this image and did there his offering; and then he leapt on his horse, and all his lords, and so the king rode toward London; and when he had ridden a little way, on the left hand there was a way to pass without London.

The same proper morning Wat Tyler, Jack Straw and John Ball had assembled their company to common together in a place called Smithfield, whereas every Friday there is a market of horses; and there were together all of affinity more than twenty thousand, and yet there were many still in the town, drinking and making merry in the taverns and paid nothing, for they were happy that made them best cheer. And these people in Smithfield had with them the king's banners, the which were delivered them the day before, and all these gluttons were in mind to overrun and to rob London the same day; for their captains said how they had done nothing as yet. 'These liberties that the king hath given us is to us but a small profit: therefore let us be all of one accord and let us overrun this rich and puissant city, or they of Essex, of Sussex, of Cambridge, of Bedford, of Arundel, of Warwick, of Reading, of Oxford, of Guildford, of Lynn, of Stafford, of Yarmouth, of Lincoln, of York and of Durham do come hither. For all these will come hither; Baker and Lister will bring them hither; and if we be first lords of London and have the possession of the riches that is therein, we shall not repent us; for if we leave it, they that come after will have it from us.'

To this counsel they all agreed; and therewith the king came the same way unware of them, for he had thought to have passed that way without London, and with him a forty horse. And when he came before the abbey of Saint Bartholomew and beheld all these people, then the king rested and said how he would go no farther till he knew what these people ailed, saying, if they were in any trouble, how he would rappease them again. The lords that were with him tarried also, as reason was when they saw the king tarry. And when Wat Tyler saw the king tarry, he said to his people: 'Sirs, yonder is the king: I will go and speak with him. Stir not from hence, without I make you a sign; and when I make you that sign, come on and slay all them except the king; but do the king no hurt, he is young, we shall do with him as we list and shall lead him with us all about England, and so shall we be lords of all the realm without doubt.' And there was a doublet-maker of London called John Tycle, and he had brought to these gluttons a sixty doublets, the which they ware: then he demanded of these captains who should pay him for his doublets; he demanded thirty mark. Wat Tyler answered him and said: 'Friend, appease yourself, thou shalt be well paid or this day be ended. Keep thee near me; I shall be thy creditor.' And therewith he spurred his horse and departed from his company and came to the king, so near him that his horse head touched the croup of the king's horse, and the first word that he said was this: 'Sir king, seest thou all yonder people?' 'Yea truly,' said the king, 'wherefore sayest thou?' 'Because,' said he, 'they be all at my commandment and have sworn to me faith and truth, to do all that I will have them' 'In a good time,' said the king, 'I will well it be so.'

Then Wat Tyler said, as he that nothing demanded but riot: 'What believest thou, king, that these people and as many more as be in London at my commandment, that they will depart from thee thus without having thy letters?' 'No,' said the king, 'ye shall have them: they be ordained for you and shall be delivered every one each after other. Wherefore, good fellows, withdraw fair and easily to your people and cause them to depart out of London; for it is our intent that each of you by villages and townships shall have letters patents, as I have promised you.'

With those words Wat Tyler cast his eyen on a squire that was there with the king bearing the king's sword, and Wat Tyler hated greatly the same squire, for the same squire had displeased him before for words between them. 'What,' said Tyler, 'art thou there? Give me thy dagger.' 'Nay,' said the squire, 'that will I not do: wherefore should I give it thee?' The king beheld the squire and said: 'Give it him; let him have it.' And so the squire took it him sore against his will. And when this Wat Tyler had it, he began to play therewith and turned it in his hand, and said again to the squire: 'Give me also that sword.' 'Nay,' said the squire, 'it is the king's sword: thou art not worthy to have it, for thou art but a knave; and if there were no more here but thou and I, thou durst not speak those words for as much gold in quantity as all yonder abbey.' 'By my faith,' said Wat Tyler, 'I shall never eat meat till I have thy head': and with those words the mayor of London came to the king with a twelve horses well armed under their coats, and so he brake the press and saw and heard how Wat Tyler demeaned himself, and said to him: 'Ha, thou knave, how art thou so hardy in the king's presence to speak such words? It is too much for thee so to do.' Then the king began to chafe and said to the mayor: 'Set hands on him.' And while the king said so, Tyler said to the mayor: 'A God's name what have I said to displease thee?' 'Yes truly,' quoth the mayor, 'thou false stinking knave, shalt thou speak thus in the presence of the king my natural lord? I commit never to live, without thou shalt dearly abye it.' And with those words the mayor drew out his sword and strake Tyler so great a stroke on the head, that he fell down at the feet of his horse, and as soon as he was fallen, they environed him all about, whereby he was not seen of his company. Then a squire of the king's alighted, called John Standish, and he drew out his sword and put it into Wat Tyler's belly, and so he died.

Then the ungracious people there assembled, perceiving their captain slain, began to murmur among themselves and said: 'Ah, our captain is slain, let us go and slay them all': and therewith they arranged themselves on the place in manner of battle, and their bows before them. Thus the king began a great outrage; howbeit, all turned to the best: for as soon as Tyler was on the earth, the king departed from all his company and all alone he rode to these people, and said to his own men: 'Sirs, none of you follow me; let me alone.' And so when he came before these ungracious people, who put themselves in ordinance to revenge their captain, then the king said to them: 'Sirs, what aileth you? Ye shall have no captain but me: I am your king: be all in rest and peace.' And so the most part of the people that heard the king speak and saw him among them, were shamefast and began to wax peaceable and to depart; but some, such as were malicious and evil, would not depart, but made semblant as though they would do somewhat.

Then the king returned to his own company and demanded of them what was best to be done. Then he was counselled to draw into the field, for to fly away was no boot. Then said the mayor: 'It is good that we do so, for I think surely we shall have shortly some comfort of them of London and of such good men as be of our part, who are purveyed and have their friends and men ready armed in their houses.' And in the mean time voice and bruit ran through London how these unhappy people were likely to slay the king and the mayor in Smithfield; through the which noise all manner of good men of the king's party issued out of their houses and lodgings well armed, and so came all to Smithfield and to the field where the king was, and they were anon to the number of seven or eight thousand men well armed. And first thither came sir Robert Knolles and sir Perducas d'Albret, well accompanied, and divers of the aldermen of London, and with them a six hundred men in harness, and a puissant man of the city, who was the king's draper, called Nicholas Bramber, and he brought with him a great company; and ever as they came, they ranged them afoot in order of battle: and on the other part these unhappy people were ready ranged, making semblance to give battle, and they had with them divers of the king's banners. There the king made three knights, the one the mayor of London sir Nicholas Walworth, sir John Standish and sir Nicholas Bramber. Then the lords said among themselves: 'What shall we do? We see here our enemies, who would gladly slay us, if they might have the better hand of us.' Sir Robert Knolles counselled to go and fight with them and slay them all; yet the king would not consent thereto, but said: 'Nay, I will not so: I will send to them commanding them to send me again my banners and thereby we shall see what they will do. Howbeit, other by fairness or otherwise, I will have them.' 'That is well said, sir,' quoth the earl of Salisbury. Then these new knights were sent to them, and these knights made token to them not to shoot at them, and when they came so near them that their speech might be heard, they said: 'Sirs, the king commandeth you to send to him again his banners, and we think he will have mercy of you.' And incontinent they delivered again the banners and sent them to the king. Also they were commanded on pain of their heads, that all such as had letters of the king to bring them forth and to send them again to the king; and so many of them delivered their letters, but not all. Then the king made them to be all to-torn in their presence; and as soon as the king's banners were delivered again, these unhappy people kept none array, but the most part of them did cast down their bows, and so brake their array and returned into London. Sir Robert Knolles was sore displeased in that he might not go to slay them all: but the king would not consent thereto, but said he would be revenged of them well enough; and so he was after.

Thus these foolish people departed, some one way and some another; and the king and his lords and all his company right ordinately entered into London with great joy. And the first journey that the king made he went to the lady princess his mother, who was in a castle in the Royal called the Queen's Wardrobe, and there she had tarried two days and two nights right sore abashed, as she had good reason; and when she saw the king her son, she was greatly rejoiced and said: 'Ah, fair son, what pain and great sorrow that I have suffered for you this day!' Then the king answered and said: 'Certainly, madam, I know it well; but now rejoice yourself and thank God, for now it is time. I have this day recovered mine heritage and the realm of England, the which I had near lost.' Thus the king tarried that day with his mother, and every lord went peaceably to their own lodgings. Then there was a cry made in every street in the king's name, that all manner of men, not being of the city of London and have not dwelt there the space of one year, to depart; and if any such be found there the Sunday by the sun-rising, that they should be taken as traitors to the king and to lose their heads. This cry thus made, there was none that durst brake it, and so all manner of people departed and sparkled abroad every man to their own places. John Ball and Jack Straw were found in an old house hidden, thinking to have stolen away, but they could not, for they were accused by their own men. Of the taking of them the king and his lords were glad, and then strake off their heads and Wat Tyler's also, and they were set on London bridge, and the valiant men's heads taken down that they had set on the Thursday before. These tidings anon spread abroad, so that the people of the strange countries, which were coming towards London, returned back again to their own houses and durst come no farther.

How the duke of Lancaster kept himself still in Scotland for fear of this rebellion, and how the king punished of these traitors the chief masters.

SUMMARY.—The duke of Lancaster concluded the treaty with the Scots and returned. On his way he was refused admittance to the town of Berwick, and hearing bad news of the rebellion, returned into Scotland to wait till better tidings came. He was singularly hated by the rebels, who spread abroad that he was a traitor to the realm. The chapter continues thus:—

Now I shall shew you the vengeance that the king of England took of these ungracious people in the mean season, while the duke of Lancaster was in Scotland.

When these people were rappeased and that Baker was executed to death, and Lister of Stafford, Wat Tyler, Jack Straw, John Ball and divers other at London, then the king was counselled to go visit his realm, through every shire, bailiwick and village, to purge and punish all the said evil-doers, and to get again all such letters as by force he had given them in divers places, and so to bring again his realm in good order. Then the king sent secretly for a certain number of men of arms to come to him at a day appointed, and so they did to the number of a five hundred spears and as many archers; and when they were all come as the king had devised, the king departed from London with his household-men all only and took the way into Kent, whereas first these ungracious people began to stir: and these foresaid men of war followed after the king and coasted him, but they rode not in his company. The king entered into Kent and came to a village called Ospringe, and called the mayor and all the men of the town before him. And when they were all come into a fair place, the king made to be shewed them by one of his council how they had erred against the king, and how they had near turned all England to tribulation and to loss. And because that the king knew well that this business was begun by some of them and not by all, wherefore it were better that some did bear the blame than all, therefore he commanded them that they should shew what they were that were culpable, on pain to be for ever in the king's indignation and to be reputed as traitors against him. And when they that were there assembled heard that request and saw well that such as were culpable should excuse all the other, then they beheld each other and at last said: 'Sir, behold him here by whom this town was first moved.' Incontinent he was taken and hanged, and so there were hanged to the number of seven; and the letters that the king had given them were demanded again, and so they were delivered again, and torn and broken before all the people. And it was said to them all: 'Sirs, ye that be here assembled, we command you in the king's name on pain of death every man to go home to his own house peaceably, and never to grudge nor rise against the king nor none of his officers; and this trespass that ye have done the king doth pardon you thereof.' Then they cried all with one voice: 'God thank the king's grace and all his council!'

In like manner as the king did at Ospringe, he did at Canterbury, at Sandwich, at Yarmouth, at Orwell and in other places in Kent: in like wise he did in all other places of his realm, whereas any rebellion had been; and there were hanged and beheaded more than fifteen hundred. Then the king was counselled to send for his uncle the duke of Lancaster out of Scotland: so the king sent for him by a knight of his house called sir Nicholas Carnefell. The knight rode so long that he came to Edinbro', and there he found the duke and his company and delivered his letters of credence from the king. The duke obeyed, as it was reason, and also gladly he would return into England to his own heritage, and so took his way to come to Roxburgh; and at his departing he thanked the lords of Scotland of the comfort that they had done to him, as in sustaining him in their realm as long as it pleased him. The earl Douglas, the earl Moray and other of Scotland brought him to the abbey of Melrose. Thus the duke came to Roxburgh and to Newcastle-upon-Tyne, and so to Durham and to York, and in every place he found cities and towns ready apparelled, as it was reason.

Dickens' Account of the Peasants' Revolt

Charles Dickens gives a more modern and sympathetic view of the rebels in his Child's History of England.

Richard, son of the Black Prince, a boy eleven years of age, succeeded to the Crown under the title of King Richard the Second. The whole English nation were ready to admire him for the sake of his brave father. As to the lords and ladies about the Court, they declared him to be the most beautiful, the wisest, and the best—even of princes—whom the lords and ladies about the Court, generally declare to be the most beautiful, the wisest, and the best of mankind. To flatter a poor boy in this base manner was not a very likely way to develop whatever good was in him; and it brought him to anything but a good or happy end.

The Duke of Lancaster, the young King's uncle—commonly called John of Gaunt, from having been born at Ghent, which the common people so pronounced—was supposed to have some thoughts of the throne himself; but, as he was not popular, and the memory of the Black Prince was, he submitted to his nephew.

The war with France being still unsettled, the Government of England wanted money to provide for the expenses that might arise out of it; accordingly a certain tax, called the Poll-tax, which had originated in the last reign, was ordered to be levied on the people. This was a tax on every person in the kingdom, male and female, above the age of fourteen, of three groats (or three four-penny pieces) a year; clergymen were charged more, and only beggars were exempt.

I have no need to repeat that the common people of England had long been suffering under great oppression. They were still the mere slaves of the lords of the land on which they lived, and were on most occasions harshly and unjustly treated. But, they had begun by this time to think very seriously of not bearing quite so much; and, probably, were emboldened by that French insurrection I mentioned in the last chapter.

The people of Essex rose against the Poll-tax, and being severely handled by the government officers, killed some of them. At this very time one of the tax-collectors, going his rounds from house to house, at

Dartford in Kent came to the cottage of one **Wat**, a tiler by trade, and claimed the tax upon his daughter. Her mother, who was at home, declared that she was under the age of fourteen; upon that, the collector (as other collectors had already done in different parts of England) behaved in a savage way, and brutally insulted Wat Tyler's daughter. The daughter screamed, the mother screamed. Wat the Tiler, who was at work not far off, ran to the spot, and did what any honest father under such provocation might have done—struck the collector dead at a blow.

Instantly the people of that town uprose as one man. They made Wat Tyler their leader; they joined with the people of Essex, who were in arms under a priest called **Jack Straw**; they took out of prison another priest named **John Ball**; and gathering in numbers as they went along, advanced, in a great confused army of poor men, to Blackheath. It is said that they wanted to abolish all property, and to declare all men equal. I do not think this very likely; because they stopped the travellers on the roads and made them swear to be true to King Richard and the people. Nor were they at all disposed to injure those who had done them no harm, merely because they were of high station; for, the King's mother, who had to pass through their camp at Blackheath, on her way to her young son, lying for safety in the Tower of London, had merely to kiss a few dirty-faced rough-bearded men who were noisily fond of royalty, and so got away in perfect safety. Next day the whole mass marched on to London Bridge.

There was a drawbridge in the middle, which **William Walworth** the Mayor caused to be raised to prevent their coming into the city; but they soon terrified the citizens into lowering it again, and spread themselves, with great uproar, over the streets. They broke open the prisons; they burned the papers in Lambeth Palace; they destroyed the **Duke of Lancaster's** Palace, the Savoy, in the Strand, said to be the most beautiful and splendid in England; they set fire to the books and documents in the Temple; and made a great riot. Many of these outrages were committed in drunkenness; since those citizens, who had well-filled cellars, were only too glad to throw them open to save the rest of their property; but even the drunken rioters were very careful to steal nothing. They were so angry with one man, who was seen to take a silver cup at the Savoy Palace, and put it in his breast, that they drowned him in the river, cup and all.

The young King had been taken out to treat with them before they committed these excesses; but, he and the people about him were so frightened by the riotous shouts, that they got back to the Tower in the best way they could. This made the insurgents bolder; so they went on rioting away, striking off the heads of those who did not, at a moment's notice, declare for King Richard and the people; and killing as many of the unpopular persons whom they supposed to be their enemies as they could by any means lay hold of. In this manner they passed one very violent day, and then proclamation was made that the King would meet them at Mile-end, and grant their requests.

The rioters went to Mile-end to the number of sixty thousand, and the King met them there, and to the King the rioters peaceably proposed four conditions. First, that neither they, nor their children, nor any coming after them, should be made slaves any more. Secondly, that the rent of land should be fixed at a certain price in money, instead of being paid in service. Thirdly, that they should have liberty to buy and sell in all markets and public places, like other free men. Fourthly, that they should be pardoned for past offences. Heaven knows, there was nothing very unreasonable in these proposals! The young King deceitfully pretended to think so, and kept thirty clerks up, all night, writing out a charter accordingly.

Now, Wat Tyler himself wanted more than this. He wanted the entire abolition of the forest laws. He was not at Mile-end with the rest, but, while that meeting was being held, broke into the Tower of London and slew the archbishop and the treasurer, for whose heads the people had cried out loudly the day before. He and his men even thrust their swords into the bed of the Princess of Wales while the Princess was in it, to make certain that none of their enemies were concealed there.

So, Wat and his men still continued armed, and rode about the city. Next morning, the King with a small train of some sixty gentlemen—among whom was **Walworth** the Mayor—rode into Smithfield, and saw Wat and his people at a little distance. Says Wat to his men, 'There is the King. I will go speak with him, and tell him what we want.'

Straightway Wat rode up to him, and began to talk. 'King,' says Wat, 'dost thou see all my men there?'

'Ah,' says the King. 'Why?'

'Because,' says Wat, 'they are all at my command, and have sworn to do whatever I bid them.'

Some declared afterwards that as Wat said this, he laid his hand on the King's bridle. Others declared that he was seen to play with his own dagger. I think, myself, that he just spoke to the King like a rough, angry man as he was, and did nothing more. At any rate he was expecting no attack, and preparing for no resistance, when Walworth the Mayor did the not very valiant deed of drawing a short sword and stabbing him in the throat. He dropped from his horse, and one of the King's people speedily finished him. So fell Wat Tyler. Fawners and flatterers made a mighty triumph of it, and set up a cry which will occasionally find an echo to this day. But Wat was a hard-working man, who had suffered much, and had been foully outraged; and it is probable that he was a man of a much higher nature and a much braver spirit than any of the parasites who exulted then, or have exulted since, over his defeat.

Seeing Wat down, his men immediately bent their bows to avenge his fall. If the young King had not had presence of mind at that dangerous moment, both he and the Mayor to boot, might have followed Tyler pretty fast. But the King riding up to the crowd, cried out that Tyler was a traitor, and that he would be their leader. They were so taken by surprise, that they set up a great shouting, and followed the boy until he was met at Islington by a large body of soldiers.

The end of this rising was the then usual end. As soon as the King found himself safe, he unsaid all he had said, and undid all he had done; some fifteen hundred of the rioters were tried (mostly in Essex) with great rigour, and executed with great cruelty. Many of them were hanged on gibbets, and left there as a terror to the country people; and, because their miserable friends took some of the bodies down to bury, the King ordered the rest to be chained up—which was the beginning of the barbarous custom of hanging in chains. The King's falsehood in this business makes such a pitiful figure, that I think Wat Tyler appears in history as beyond comparison the truer and more respectable man of the two.

Richard was now sixteen years of age, and married Anne of Bohemia, an excellent princess, who was called 'the good Queen Anne.'

She deserved a better husband; for the King had been fawned and flattered into a treacherous, wasteful, dissolute, bad young man.

There were two Popes at this time (as if one were not enough!), and their quarrels involved Europe in a great deal of trouble. Scotland was still troublesome too; and at home there was much jealousy and distrust, and plotting and counter-plotting, because the King feared the ambition of his relations, and particularly of his uncle, the Duke of Lancaster, and the duke had his party against the King, and the King had his party against the duke. Nor were these home troubles lessened when the duke went to Castile to urge his claim to the crown of that kingdom; for then the Duke of Gloucester, another of Richard's uncles, opposed him, and influenced the Parliament to demand the dismissal of the King's favourite ministers. The King said in reply, that he would not for such men dismiss the meanest servant in his kitchen. But, it had begun to signify little what a King said when a Parliament was determined; so Richard was at last obliged to give way, and to agree to another Government of the kingdom, under a commission of fourteen nobles, for a year. His uncle of Gloucester was at the head of this commission, and, in fact, appointed everybody composing it.

Having done all this, the King declared as soon as he saw an opportunity that he had never meant to do it, and that it was all illegal; and he got the judges secretly to sign a declaration to that effect. The secret oozed out directly, and was carried to the Duke of Gloucester. The Duke of Gloucester, at the head of forty thousand men, met the King on his entering into London to enforce his authority; the King was helpless against him; his favourites and ministers were impeached and were mercilessly executed. Among them were two men whom the people regarded with very different feelings; one, Robert Tresilian, Chief Justice, who was hated for having made what was called 'the bloody circuit' to try the rioters; the other, Sir Simon Burley, an honourable knight, who had been the dear friend of the Black Prince, and the governor and guardian of the King. For this gentleman's life the good Queen even begged of Gloucester on her knees; but Gloucester (with or without reason) feared and hated him, and replied, that if she valued her husband's crown, she had better beg no more. All this was done under what was called by some the wonderful—and by others, with better reason, the merciless—Parliament.

More Early English Drama from the Groundling Press

Anonymous
The Life and Death of Jack Straw
The Peasants' Revolt of 1381 is one of the great watershed events in English history. This anonymous sixteenth-century play follows the rebels as they march on London to confront the young Richard II.

Richard Brome
The Weeding of Covent Garden *(in preparation)*
Brome's "city comedy" features a wild cast of drunken Puritans and swordfighting prostitutes, disguised fathers and scheming sons, in the new and controversial neighborhood of Covent Garden.

For more information on the Groundling Press editions, please visit us at:

www.groundlingpress.com

Manufactured by Amazon.ca
Acheson, AB

14012709R00055